automating
hydroponics

for kitchen gardeners to greenhouse growers

BASIC SYSTEMS TO FULL TECH • FRESH FOOD YEAR-ROUND

Cerreto Rossouw

GroundSwell Books
Summertown, Tennessee

Library of Congress Cataloging-in-Publication Data
is available upon request.

We chose to print this title on responsibly harvested paper
stock certified by the Forest Stewardship Council, an
independent auditor of responsible forestry practices. For
more information, visit us.fsc.org.

MIX
Paper from
responsible sources
FSC® C005010

Cover and interior design: John Wincek
Stock photography: 123 RF

Printed in the United States of America

GroundSwell Books
an imprint of Book Publishing Company
PO Box 99
Summertown, TN 38483
888-260-8458
bookpubco.com

ISBN: 978-1-57067-366-5

23 22 21 20 19 18   1 2 3 4 5 6 7 8 9

This book is for educational purposes
only. Although every precaution has
been taken to verify the accuracy of
the information contained in this book,
the author and publisher assume no
responsibility for any errors or omissions
and disclaim any liability to any party
for any loss or damage, whether from
accident, negligence, disruption, or any
other cause that may result from the
use of the information provided herein.

contents

list of illustrations

FIGURES

TABLES

automating
hydroponics

for kitchen gardeners to greenhouse growers

BASIC SYSTEMS TO FULL TECH • FRESH FOOD YEAR-ROUND

introduction

Hydroponic farming is a great way to grow top-quality food using less space, and at a faster rate than soil-based farming and for a lower cost than store-bought produce. It can be as simple or as complicated as you are comfortable with and can easily be scaled from a small home-based greenhouse to a large-production hydroponic farm.

With rising food costs and the spread of world hunger, there's no better time than right now to start growing your own food at home. You can even sell your excess crops to neighbors or the local grocery store.

Farming has become a forgotten skill in our modern society. It's misconstrued as a time-consuming, labor-intensive process, requiring a talented green thumb, a huge allocation of capital, and lots of acres of land. This is certainly not true.

Hydroponic crop yields are between five and ten times greater using the same space as soil-based crops. Hydroponic farming also uses 90 percent less water than conventional farming, and since the plants are only given the exact nutrients they need, costs are significantly reduced. Depending on the particular hydroponic setup, pesticides can be nearly eliminated, since the growing environment is enclosed.

Hydroponic farming makes vertical farming possible, which results in abundant yields and rapid growth, and makes it possible for a typical family to supply all their fruit and vegetable needs from their own backyard. The exact amount of space required depends on the type of crops that are planted and the size of the family, but even if you just supplement your current needs, it would be a terrific start.

There are also environmental benefits. The carbon footprint for your food can be dramatically decreased with hydroponic production, since no energy is being spent on transporting, storing, or packaging your food. You can also sidestep the lengthy list of secondary costs and energy expenditures associated with commercial food production, such as operating the stores, factories, and equipment necessary to produce and warehouse the food.

This book provides you with all the information you need to create the perfect hydroponic system to meet your individual specifications. It starts by covering the array of systems available and their variations, followed by chapters on what plants need to thrive and how to address each concern within the hydroponic system. Tables are provided for specific crop requirements, along with information on pest control and general care and maintenance. If you're more technically inclined, you can learn how to automate part or all of your hydroponic system. Depending on your budget and technical abilities, you could even limit your involvement to simply planting the seeds and harvesting your crops when they're ready!

I grow plants for many reasons:
to please my eye or to please my soul,
to challenge the elements or to challenge my patience,
for novelty or for nostalgia,
but mostly for the joy in seeing them grow.

DAVID HOBSON

1

hydroponic systems

The glory of gardening: hands in the dirt, head in the sun, heart with nature.
To nurture a garden is to feed not just the body, but the soul.

ALFRED AUSTIN

all hydroponic systems have a few things in common. They create the ideal environment for plants to grow, supplying just the right amounts of light, water, and nutrients. They also don't use soil, although a chemically neutral growing medium is typically used to anchor the roots or retain water when needed.

You don't have to choose a single hydroponic system. Instead, you can use the best ones for the crops you have selected. It's relatively simple to maintain a large variety of plants in the same growing area, provided you group plants with similar requirements together. Plants that differ too much will need their own separate nutrient-solution reservoirs.

Nutrient Film Technique (NFT)

This system is probably the most popular one and comes in a variety of configurations. It typically consists of PVC piping with holes drilled on top into which plastic mesh pots containing a growing medium (not soil) are placed to hold the plants. The roots of the plants grow through the mesh pots and into the PVC piping, where a trickling stream of water runs, containing the exact concentration of nutrients that the plants need at that particular time.

The water containing the nutrient mixture is held in a reservoir, and a water pump is used to pump it into the PVC system. The water runs along the inside of the PVC pipe, across the roots, and then back into the reservoir. A minimum sloping of 1 inch

(25 mm) per 3.28 feet (1 m) is required to prevent water from pooling in the PVC pipe. A water flow rate of 1 quart (1 L) per minute is recommended.

A strong air pump connected to an air stone is used to oxygenate the water by disrupting the water surface. Chapter 5 (page 68) discusses other methods to add more agitation to the water.

I recommend using a PVC pipe with the largest diameter that makes the most financial sense. A diameter of 4 inches (10 cm) might be fine for plants with small root systems, but a minimum of 6 inches (15 cm) for general usage is best.

The typical planting distance between medium-sized crops should be 12 inches (30 cm). For smaller crops, such as herbs, this distance can be decreased to 4 inches (10 cm) or even less. The crops should be planted as close together as possible without affecting their light supply. For this reason, I recommend having PVC pipes with various hole distances; otherwise, use a 4-inch (10-cm) hole distance throughout the system and leave some holes open if more space is required. If an 8-inch (20-cm) minimum distance is required, leave every other hole open. If you need a 12-inch (30-cm) distance, only use every third hole.

Figure 1.1 (on the following page) shows a basic NFT system. This system can incorporate some of the elements of other systems to improve performance. For example, the system described so far doesn't allow for seeds to be planted directly into the mesh pots, since an established root system is required to reach the nutrient solution. This means additional labor.

Instead, the Wick System (see pages 10–11) can offer a solution to this problem. You can thread a piece of cotton rope through the mesh pot close to the seed, which will draw up the nutrient solution to the seed. It acts as a temporary root system for seeds and seedlings until they can reach the nutrient solution on their own. The wick can remain in the system until the crop is replaced.

Another option is to run the irrigation pipe all the way through the length of the PVC pipe (instead of terminating it at

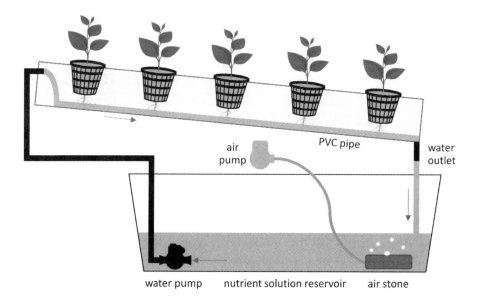

air pump

PVC pipe

water outlet

water pump   nutrient solution reservoir   air stone

FIG. 1.1 Basic NFT system

the top entrance of the PVC pipe system) and attach micro spray nozzles next to each mesh pot. Water is sprayed directly onto the growing medium inside the mesh pot. This works well for growing mediums that can retain water so the water can reach the seeds. The unused nutrient solution will drip down to the PVC pipe and return to the reservoir. These improvements borrow elements from the aeroponic system (see pages 13–15).

Similarly, you can borrow a concept from yet another method called the drip system (see pages 11–13). This method relies on dripping the nutrient solution at the base of the plant or directly above the seed. No spray nozzle is required for the drip system, but some one-directional nozzles will work well. In this scenario, the irrigation line runs on the outside of the PVC pipe, with a nozzle or dripper for each plant.

If you're going to stick to the vanilla approach and rely on the root system to directly soak up the nutrients from the water trickling down the PVC pipe, I recommend that you use a square pipe instead of a round pipe and ensure that the water creates an even film at the bottom instead of trickling down one area. This will give the roots more surface contact from which to collect nutrients.

Note that all PVC systems are prone to overgrown roots, which could choke off the nutrient supply to other plants. Any of the improvements I described should help with this, but it's also important to prevent pooling of water in the system, as this could cause problems such as root rot.

If you only use the PVC pipe to drain away excess nutrients (such as the two improvements that use irrigation lines for each plant), you can make an additional enhancement by inserting a fine-mesh plastic strip inside the bottom area of the PVC pipe through which water can drip but that will keep out most of the roots. This will improve drainage and eliminate pooling.

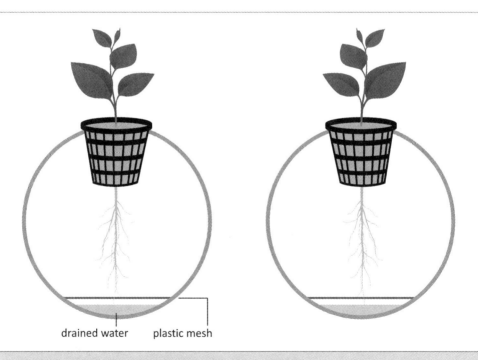

drained water   plastic mesh

FIG. 1.2 Using plastic mesh to improve draining

Multiple PVC pipes can drain to the same nutrient tank when crops are similar enough. If space isn't a problem, the pipes can be placed horizontally (parallel) at the same height. Their slopes will be in the same direction and will therefore all drain at one end.

When space is a concern, you can use an A-frame (as shown in figure 1.3), which is two upright rectangular frames standing back to back at an angle. Each rectangular frame can hold several PVC pipes. Note that the steeper the A-frame, the less sun your crops will receive, especially at the bottom. The top rows will receive full sun. Place your A-frames so that they run north to south. This will ensure that each side of the frame will receive at least 75 percent of direct sunlight if it's at a 45-degree angle (recommended), regardless of the season. If it's placed east to west, one side might not get any direct light, depending on the time of year.

If you're wondering how the amount of sun is calculated, figure 1.4 (on the following page) will explain it. It's basically equal to the outside angle of the A-frame.

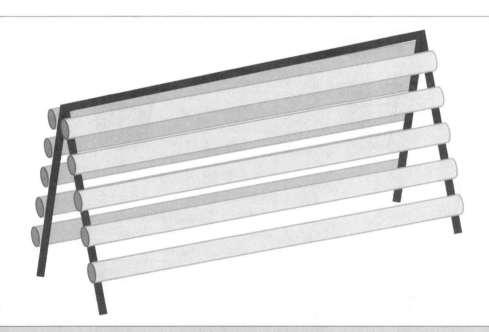

FIG. 1.3 A standard A-frame

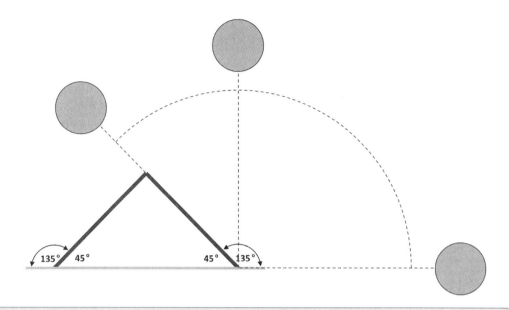

FIG. 1.4 How sunlight exposure is calculated

A helpful aspect of an A-frame is that you can add hinges to the top so you can adjust the incline as required. For crops that require more light, the frame can be lowered. If you have a greenhouse area, you can lower your A-frames so the pathway between them is eliminated when you aren't working in the greenhouse. This will slightly increase the plants' surface area that will be exposed to light. When you need to access your crops, simply raise one of the A-frames a bit. You will need to add coaster wheels so you can easily move the frames. Some coaster wheels come with a locking mechanism. This is very useful for frame stability and will prevent a collapse at more shallow angles.

Instead of an A-frame, you can use a single rectangular frame placed against a wall at an angle. Consider this option if it makes more sense in the space you are working with.

You might see some hydroponic systems in which the top PVC pipe drains to the pipe directly below it, and only the last PVC pipe drains back into the nutrient tank. I don't recommend this unless the total length of the PVC system is less than 40 feet

(12 m); otherwise, the oxygen and nutrient levels might be too low for the crops farther down in the system. For scalability and simplicity, drain each PVC pipe directly into the nutrient tank.

The flexibility of the NFT system makes it suitable for most small to medium-sized plants. It isn't suitable for larger plants, since the PVC pipe will be a limiting factor. Although large PVC pipes are available, you can obtain less-expensive systems for larger plants. There are also more cost-effective systems for plants, such as lettuce, that require large amounts of water.

Wick System

The wick system is a passive setup and doesn't use a water pump. Its concept serves as an improvement to the NFT system in terms of assisting seeds and seedlings with developing roots.

Instead of a water pump, strings of cotton rope are suspended directly into the nutrient tank. A large clay flower bed filled with a water-retaining growing medium (not soil) is used instead of the mesh pots from the NFT system. It will have several holes drilled through the bottom in a grid formation that wicks can be inserted into. Water can then be drawn up by the wicks to the plant.

The wicks should fit snugly into the holes but should not be too tight; otherwise, they might negatively affect the wicking process. Don't use a knot to prevent the wick from slipping out; instead, use small plastic pins that can be poked perpendicularly through each wick. Avoid using wood or any other degradable or chemically reactive material. Plastic toothpicks should work perfectly.

Wicks are more effective over short distances, so keep the tray close to the water (within about 2 inches/6 cm). To improve wick performance, you can unravel both ends of the cotton rope a bit to increase its surface areas at the exchange points.

The flower bed can then be used to plant crops in the same way that you would with soil, minus the need to water the crops

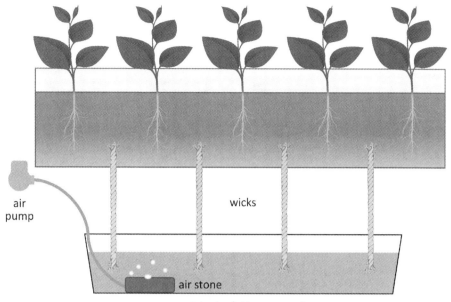

air
pump

wicks

air stone

nutrient solution reservoir

FIG. 1.5 The wick system

or spend money on a water pump. An air pump is still used to oxygenate the water.

You can control the moisture level by the number of wicks. It's better to add too many wicks rather than too few, since you can tie up some of them if the growing medium becomes too saturated with water.

This system works best with small crops, such as herbs. It uses less electricity and is one of the most inexpensive systems available. It does use more growing medium than potted systems, but the growing medium is quite economical.

Drip System

The drip system entails running an irrigation line to each plant and slowly dripping the nutrient solution near the base of the plant (see figure 1.6). This system is perfect for bigger crops,

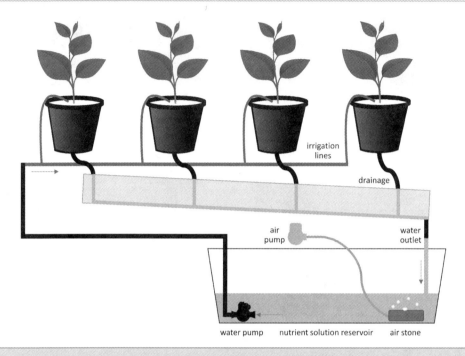

irrigation lines

drainage

air pump

water outlet

water pump   nutrient solution reservoir   air stone

FIG. 1.6 The drip system

as each plant would be placed in its own larger pot. The unused nutrient solution will drip through the base of the pot and can be returned to the nutrient tank.

The method of collection will depend on the size of the pot. Just ensure that water doesn't pool up anywhere in the system and that water is exposed to as little light as possible; otherwise, algae will start to grow. Of course, this is true for any of the other systems as well.

You can use a gutter line running below the pots to re-collect the unused nutrient solution. Alternatively, you can use a very large, shallow tray for the nutrient solution and suspend the pots directly above the solution to allow it to drip back into the nutrient tank. You will need to enclose it to eliminate light.

Another option is to drill a small hole in the bottom of each bucket and attach a drainage line to it. The drainage line could be a rubber hose or narrow plastic tube, but make sure it's sealed properly. Glue some meshed material over the hole on the inside of the pot before adding the growing medium. The mesh should be fine enough to filter out any particles of the growing medium and allow only the water to drain out.

This system affords a high level of flexibility in terms of the placement and size of the pots, since you only need to run an irrigation line to it, and there are several ways in which the excess nutrient solution can be drained and collected. However, the drip system tends to be slightly more expensive, since it requires dealing with the nutrient supply and drainage for each plant.

Aeroponic System

With the aeroponic system, the roots of the plants are suspended in the air and misting nozzles spray the nutrient solution onto the root systems. Usually no growing medium is required for this system, but it will be necessary to start the seeds in a grow tray and transplant the seedlings once they have developed a decent root system.

In my discussion of the NFT system (page 4), I suggest the concept behind this method as a possible improvement. In the scenario described, a growing medium was present, so once again, you can see how there are multiple ways in which the system could be designed.

Typically the aeroponic system would have an enclosed container, such as a very large plastic storage box with a lid. Holes would be drilled into the lid through which the plants would be suspended. To prevent the plants from falling through the holes, they should be placed in mesh pots (without any growing medium, or in growing mediums that don't retain water) or secured in some other fashion. For instance, a relatively dense foam sheet (about 1 inch/2.5 cm thick) could be fastened to the bottom of the lid. For each plant, pierce a hole in the foam using a thin rod, such as a knitting needle. The hole should be small enough to allow the foam to firmly grip the stem of the plant as it grows. This method

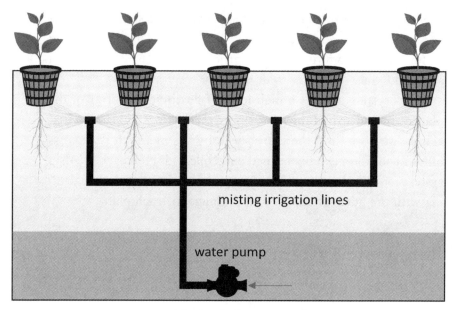

misting irrigation lines

water pump

nutrient solution reservoir

FIG. 1.7 The aeroponic system

is a less-expensive alternative to mesh pots. It's better suited for lighter, smaller plants, such as herbs, or plants with a wide base, such as lettuce. It has the advantage of allowing you to plant seeds directly into the foam, but you'll have to take care that the seeds don't fall through it. If the system's mister can reach the foam, it should be able to provide enough water for the seeds to grow without manual watering. For more details about caring for seeds and seedlings, see "Seeds and Cloning," page 30.

The plastic container should be filled about one-third of the way with the nutrient solution. Several misting nozzles will need to be attached to a pump to ensure all the roots are properly irrigated. Misting nozzles are better than spraying nozzles for aeroponic systems, and the plants will grow much better.

Any excess nutrient solution will drip back down into the container and be recycled. No air pump is required, since the water is oxygenated during misting and the roots already receive enough oxygen.

Be aware that any system that doesn't use a growing medium, or that uses a growing medium that doesn't retain water, requires the crop to be irrigated at very regular intervals to prevent the roots from drying out. The disadvantage of this is that a power failure or pump failure could ruin the crop. Also, the fine misting nozzles can clog easily, so it's a good idea to add an inline filter that can remove any particles.

Water Culture System

With the water culture system (see figure 1.8), the roots of the plants are directly suspended in the water with the nutrient solution. It's the preferred system for crops that require a lot of water, such as lettuce.

The system looks very similar to the aeroponic system (see figure 1.7, page 14), but the tank is filled much higher and no

air pump

air stone

nutrient solution reservoir

FIG. 1.8 The water culture system

water pump or misters are necessary. Instead, an air pump is used to oxygenate the water. Note that if the air pump should fail, the crop might be lost.

A Styrofoam sheet floats on top of the water's surface, taking the place of a lid. The roots of the plants are inserted through holes in the Styrofoam sheet. The sheet ensures that the roots always make full contact with the water, even when that water level fluctuates as the plants consume it.

The Ebb and Flow System

The ebb and flow system (see figure 1.9) uses two containers. One contains the plants in a growing medium, and the other one contains the nutrient solution. At regular intervals, a water pump is used to flood the container with the plants for a set

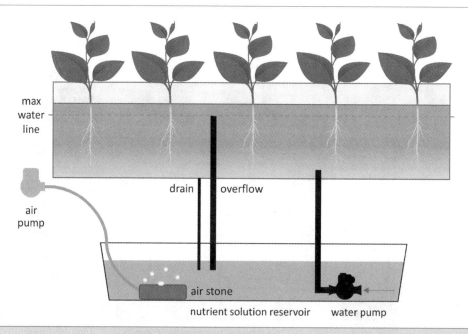

FIG. 1.9 The ebb and flow system

amount of time. A drain outlet and overflow outlet are present in the system.

A growing medium that doesn't retain water should be used for this system. It will allow for sufficient levels of oxygen to reach the roots when the container isn't flooded, and it will supply the roots with nutrients when it is flooded.

Make sure that the drain line is narrower than the pump line. The overflow must be the same diameter as the pump's line or wider. This will not only ensure that the tank doesn't drain faster than the pump can fill the tank, but also that it will not be able to fill the tank higher than the maximum waterline.

CHAPTER

2

growing area

The greatest fine art of the future will be the making
of a comfortable living from a small piece of land.

ABRAHAM LINCOLN

ow that you're aware of the various hydroponic systems available, let's take a look at your growing environment. The kind of environment you create will depend on what is most suitable for your property and your budget.

The most important aspect to keep in mind is maintaining a clean environment. The environment doesn't necessarily have to be completely sterile, but if that's doable, it would be best. For example, it's perfectly acceptable to have a small system on your kitchen windowsill to grow a few herbs to use in recipes. The kitchen is clean enough for you to maintain a small-scale system like this, and if you encounter a problem, it's not a significant loss.

The risk for complications comes into play with larger crops. For instance, a common problem is root rot. If this happens with a small system, you can simply clear out the entire setup and plant a new crop. However, it's quite a different matter if you are forced to replace an entire greenhouse full of crops.

Indoors

The first decision you'll need to make is about the scale of your system. If your intention is to grow just a few herbs or limited amounts of small fruits or vegetables, the best option would be to look at a compact indoor system that's no bigger than a wall. These types of systems are usually very cost-effective and offer a plethora of options. Since they're meant to form part of your décor, you can aim to make them aesthetically pleasing. There are many prefab systems available that offer everything you'll need straight out of the box. They will cost more than a system you build yourself, but you won't need to worry about the design and can skip right to planting your first crop.

For larger yields, designing your own system is 90 percent of the fun. Have a look online to get a few ideas for a system that would suit your needs. Some designs might provide a step-by-step guide on how to build a specific system, but if the instructions are lacking, you can at least use the online photos as a starting point for your own design.

You might be surprised how much you can grow in a small space. Even a small apartment can accommodate a small system of some sort. For example, if you have an available wall in your kitchen or somewhere else in your house (even in your living room), you could mount stylish enclosed wooden boxes. The nutrient tank, pumps, and other equipment can be hidden inside the boxes, with only the growing medium or the holes in which the plants grow exposed. You can even make it a multipurpose unit by adding cupboards or drawers.

In your kitchen, any unused wall or counter area can be an excellent spot to add a small hydroponic system. You could potentially mount small racks on the wall or suspend grow boxes from the ceiling.

Note that indoor systems will usually lack proper levels of light, so you might need to supplement with artificial lights. See page 41 for information on the various lighting options that are available.

Outdoors

If you're a more serious grower, you could build a small greenhouse in your backyard. Even a few square feet/meters could be enough to supply a significant portion or even all of the herbs, fruits, and vegetables you need.

Before you consider building a greenhouse in your backyard, investigate whether you need to register the building plans with any authorities. This will add to your costs, so find out under what circumstances you're required to do so. Depending on where you live, building plans may not be necessary if you don't need to lay a permanent foundation. In some regions, you might need to submit plans only if the greenhouse will exceed a certain size or if you use certain building materials. Other rules or building codes might also apply to your situation, so familiarize yourself with these guidelines so you can work within them and possibly avoid submitting your plans.

Building a greenhouse doesn't need to be a complicated process. It could be as simple as building a wooden frame and floor and covering it with plastic sheeting. You can include a standard external door, but if you're not going to install extractor fans, you'll need to add windows for ventilation as well. The windows don't need to be glass.

Using inexpensive wood and plastic sheeting will allow you to build a relatively large greenhouse for a surprisingly low cost. Bear in mind that you'll need to treat any wood that will be exposed to the elements. You'll also need to occasionally replace the plastic sheeting, since the sun will affect its translucency and alter the light spectrum reaching the plants. Be aware that the plastic sheeting can rupture quite easily. Fortunately, it's relatively inexpensive to replace, but it does require regular maintenance. Small holes can simply be patched with clear tape.

Purchase UV-stabilized plastic sheeting, as it will last much longer than non-stabilized sheeting. Also look for an infrared-reflective sheet with light-diffusing properties. Plants need light to grow, but they don't need the heat associated with direct sunlight, which is radiated as infrared waves. Light diffusion will scatter the light more evenly throughout the greenhouse, with very little effect on the intensity of the light available to the plants.

If you live in a very windy area, or if you're not interested in regular maintenance, plastic sheeting might not be the best option. Instead, you can use Perspex sheets or glass panes. Since these are rigid, the elements will be less of a problem. Perspex is quite durable, but it also suffers from degradation with long-term exposure to the sun. Look for the same properties as with plastic sheeting when shopping for Perspex sheeting. Glass doesn't suffer from degradation, so it's the preferred material if you want to eliminate maintenance due to sun exposure. You should still look for heat-reflective diffusing glass. Unfortunately, glass and Perspex sheeting will drastically affect your costs.

Since your greenhouse will require water and electricity, you will need to install supply lines. Note that additional regulations and building codes will come into effect when plumbing and electricity are involved. You might need to hire a plumber and electrician to handle the installations. The plumber will also need to install a gutter to properly dispose of any wastewater. It could be illegal to dump nutrient-rich water into soil because it could contaminate freshwater supplies. This is when professional advice is worth the extra expense. You don't necessarily need the electrician and plumber to deal with all your electrical and plumbing needs inside the greenhouse. They will likely only be required for installing the water supply and electricity to the greenhouse and dealing with wastewater disposal.

Layout

Once you've built your greenhouse, you'll need to decide which hydroponic systems you'd like to use. The crops you plant might play a role in your decision. If you have water-loving crops, such as lettuce, you might want to incorporate a water culture system (see page 15) in at least one area. If you plan on having large plants or small trees, you'll need individual pots, which will require the drip system (see page 11). The rest of the greenhouse can make use of one of the other systems, depending on your preference, with NFT (see page 4) being the most versatile.

Try to keep your systems mobile if possible. This will allow you to change the layout if necessary, and using A-frames (see page 8) will allow you to adjust the incline.

In small greenhouses, providing proper access to light for all crops can be a challenge. Mobile platforms will let you to rearrange the crops for optimal exposure to light. Fortunately, not all crops require the same amount of light, and this can be used to your advantage. Nonflowering leafy plants require less light, so they can be placed in lower areas with more shade.

Light

To take advantage of as much light as possible, use matte white paint to cover all wooden surfaces and containers. The paint will reflect any unused light back to the plants. The floor should also be painted matte white or be covered in white plastic sheeting. Avoid using glossy paint, as it will be less reflective. A matte white surface can reflect up to 80 percent of the light. Don't use aluminium foil, as it doesn't reflect light well; it's better suited for reflecting heat. Mylar is a relatively inexpensive, highly reflective (up to 95 percent) plastic sheet, making it good for covering the floor.

Use white PVC piping, but ensure that it's thick enough to maintain a completely dark environment inside the PVC pipe; if the water is exposed to any light, algae will grow in it. Some PVC pipes are white on the outside and painted black on the inside, so be on the lookout for those. Make sure you buy UV-stabilized PVC pipes, as the UV stabilization will prevent the pipes from cracking when they're exposed to the sun for lengthy periods.

If you can't get hold of any heat-reflecting glass or plastic sheeting, you'll need to include some shade netting for plants that don't do well in direct sunlight. Alternatively, you could use electronic blinds to control direct light exposure, depending on how high-tech you want your system to be.

General Care

Remember that a hydroponic greenhouse must be kept as sterile as possible. This means taking the following extra precautions:

1. **Properly seal the greenhouse.** No insects should be able to enter the greenhouse, so any cracks and gaps should be sealed with silicone. Adding rubber strips to the door and window frames will provide an almost airtight seal. Test your greenhouse with a water hose to ensure that you didn't miss any cracks.

2. **Ventilate the greenhouse by opening windows.** Put mesh screens or mosquito netting over the windows to allow airflow but prevent insects from entering. The screens or netting might not provide total protection, but they will definitely help and will be better than having nothing at all. If you have extractor fans (which I highly recommend), add filters and clean them regularly.

3. **Add inline filters to all your nutrient tanks.** Inline filters will prevent any spray nozzles or irrigation tubes from clogging. Just remember to clean them regularly; otherwise, they will add additional strain to the water pump.

4. **Take care when entering the greenhouse.** Make sure you don't accidentally let in any insects, soil, or debris, such as leaves. If you live in a windy area, add a double-door system so you can enter the first door, clean off your shoes, and then enter through the second door.

5. **Never introduce soil in the hydroponic garden.** Even house-plants should be exiled. In addition, never transplant any plant into a hydroponic system that grew in any form of soil. Doing so will introduce soil-related pathogens and could con-taminate the entire greenhouse.

6. **Sterilize your tools and equipment.** All tools and equipment, such as pruners and hand shovels, should be sterilized before

being used and should only be used in the hydroponic garden. Purchase a separate set of tools and equipment for your soil garden. It's also a good idea to wear gloves.

7. **Take advantage of having multiple nutrient tanks.** Even though hydroponic systems are sensitive to contamination, they use multiple separate nutrient tanks, which is advantageous. If you see a problem with one crop from a specific nutrient tank, you can deal with the problem immediately and prevent it from spreading throughout the entire greenhouse. For this to work, though, you must first ensure that you aren't the cause of cross-contamination, so give your equipment a quick cleaning when you switch crops from different nutrient tanks.

8. **Remove dead plant material every day.** One of the daily checks you'll need to do is to look for dead plant material and prune any unhealthy or browning leaves and branches. There's no need for the plant to spend energy on parts that won't contribute to its well-being. Even more important, removing decay will prevent pathogens from growing.

9. **Check the health of the root system.** Any browning of the roots could indicate a problem. You can trim off unhealthy roots, but be very careful when working with the root system because it's extremely sensitive. If only one plant is affected, it might be a good call to pull it from the system and dispose of it. Make sure you get all its roots. If all roots in the system are turning brown, there might be a problem with the nutrient solution. On page 72, I discuss how to properly maintain your nutrient solution, but if that fails, you might need to flush the tank, sterilize it, and start a new batch. If browning continues, you must dispose of the entire crop for that tank and restart with a new nutrient batch.

10. **Avoid overgrown roots.** Roots can easily become overgrown, which could prevent proper water flow and cause the stagna-

tion of water. This can become a breeding ground for water-based pathogens. Check your PVC pipes or containers regularly and trim any problematic roots. In a hydroponic system, large root systems aren't useful, since nutrients are delivered directly to them. Plants need to focus their growth elsewhere instead of wasting their resources on roots.

11. **Prune each plant to control its growing area.** If a plant starts to grow too wide or too high, it needs to be trimmed so it can focus its energy on the space you have reserved for it.

12. **Use the right fertilizer.** Never use any fertilizer that isn't specifically formulated for hydroponics. All fertilizers used for soil-based plants are unsuitable for hydroponic systems.

Pest Control

I f you keep the growing area sealed and sterile, you won't need to rely on pesticides very often. When you eat commercial crops, you're consuming pesticides in one form or another, even if you choose organic produce. Remember that organic farming doesn't mean that pesticides aren't used.

Nevertheless, even in a sterile environment you might encounter some pest problems from time to time. These could range from a fungus outbreak to an infestation of mites or other insects.

Although it's best to avoid using pesticides, there are a few that are suitable for use in a hydroponic environment when needed. Try to prevent any pesticide from reaching the water; that way you can minimize your exposure when you consume the crop.

If you monitor your greenhouse very frequently, you will be able to spot issues as soon as they pop up. If the problem hasn't spread to other crops, you could consider just removing the affected plants. By sacrificing the affected plants, you can steer clear of pesticides while effectively containing the problem.

An alternative to pesticides is to use beneficial predatory insects. These insects aren't interested in your crop and only target the pests you're trying to get rid of. As soon as the pests have been dealt with, the predatory insects start to die off due to lack of food, leaving you with a pest-free and insect-free growing area. An example of a very useful insect for pest control is the ladybug (also known as the ladybird). You can purchase ladybugs in large quantities if you have a sizable greenhouse or if you're unable obtain them by any other means. Another useful creature is the predatory spider mite. It hunts and eradicates any plant spider mites it encounters. Predatory spider mites will eventually die from starvation once the plant spider mites have been eliminated.

Certain plants are also very useful for pest control. These include bittersweet, cinnamon, citronella, derris, garlic, lemongrass, neem, and tomatoes. Reserve some space in your growing area for these plants so you can reduce the number of pests you might encounter.

Search online for additional ways to identify your pest problem and find the best method to resolve it. Seek out methods that can eliminate the infestation without pesticides. There are almost always safe and effective alternatives.

Pollination

S ome plants are self-pollinating, but others rely on the wind or insects for assistance. Work with self-pollinating varieties whenever possible. Those that rely on the wind may need to be subjected to a strong fan or possibly multiple fans, depending on the size of your greenhouse.

If you have plants that rely on insects, you'll need to manually pollinate the plants or introduce some pollinating insects, such as bees, butterflies, or moths. It's fine to bring these beneficial insects into your greenhouse, but if the space you have isn't big enough, it might not be able to sustain them. You would also need to keep an eye out for dead insects and remove them as soon as possible. Bees are the most popular insect choice, but their stingers can be a problem for gardeners.

Luckily, if you opt for pollinating the flowers yourself, the process is very simple. All you'll need is a soft brush, such as a makeup brush. You can then just brush each flower in a twisting manner. If your greenhouse isn't very big, this won't be a very time-consuming process.

seeds and cloning

If you have a garden and a library, you have everything you need.

MARCUS TULLIUS CICERO

t his chapter briefly covers the most important things you need to know about sprouting seeds and how to transplant them in your hydroponic system. You'll also learn how to clone your favorite plants.

Seeds

Y ou don't need special seed variants for growing your own crops hydroponically. As mentioned on page 28, if you can choose among multiple variants, select those that are self-pollinating.

Hydroponic growers generally prefer germinating their seeds in a grow tray and transplanting the seedlings when they have a well-developed root system. That's because the grow medium isn't as dense as soil, so a seed could potentially be washed away. Another reason is that hydroponic systems are designed to provide water and nutrients to a root system. The seeds often won't receive any water unless a few modifications are made to the system. For example, with NFT, water wouldn't be able to reach the seed area unless the system is fitted with a misting irrigation line, a drip line, or a wick for each net pot.

Planting your seeds directly into the hydroponic system is possible with just a few modifications. In addition, you would need a way to secure the seed in place. A great solution is to use small sponge cubes; even the sponges found in some medicine bottles will work. A thickness of about 1 inch (2–3 cm) is recommended. Make a small incision of ¼–½ inch (1–2 cm) in the middle of each sponge cube with a sharp crafting knife or scalpel. The cut should go straight through the sponge, but the incision at the bottom can be much smaller. Cut another slit perpendicular to the first incision to form a cross (see figure 3.1 on the facing page). When you're done, you shouldn't be able to see through the sponge. The incision should close on its own, so don't cut a visible hole through it.

The seed can then be placed into the incision at a depth of ¼–½ inch (1–2 cm). Test its stability by pouring a glass of water over it. If the seed doesn't flush out, you'll be able to use it in your hydroponic system.

If the system you use is capable of supplying the seed with

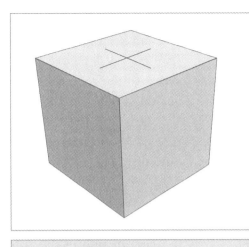

FIG. 3.1 A scored sponge cube

water, the seed will be able to germinate, and the roots will grow through the bottom of the sponge cube. The cube itself won't interfere with the plant, so there's no reason to remove it at a later stage.

To make sure that each bay in your system will have a plant, you'll need to place two or three seeds in each sponge cube. That's because not all seeds will germinate. The expected percentage is usually disclosed on the seed packet.

Once the seeds germinate and the seedlings have grown a bit, some cubes will have more than one seedling. Keep the strongest-looking seedling in each cube and cut away or pull out any others. Be careful not to harm the healthy ones when pulling out the others.

You can plant seeds directly into finer water-retaining growing mediums. For example, the drip system (page 11) and wick system (page 10) use large pots or clay flower beds filled with a growing medium that would be suitable for planting seeds without the need for seed trays or sponge cubes.

Using a seed tray has some advantages because you can create an environment more suitable for seeds. For instance, seed sprouting can be accelerated by putting a heating mat under the tray. You can also have better quality control; that's because you can germinate about 20 percent more seeds than you'll need, so you can keep only the strongest seedlings. Any pods with more than one seedling can be easily removed since you'll have ready access to the root system, and you can make sure that only the healthiest one remains in each cube.

Seeds and the root system of seedlings prefer a temperature of 71–80 degrees F (22–27 degrees C) with 100 percent humidity. The air temperature should be 68–77 degrees F (20–25 degrees C) with 70–90 percent humidity. You can speed up the germination process by presoaking the seeds in a 10 percent hydroperoxide solution.

The strength of the nutrient solution for seedlings should be only 50 percent. Once they have two to four sets of proper leaves, you can use a full-strength solution. Around this stage they'll be ready to be transplanted into your hydroponic system. Transplanting is a stressful experience for the plants, and their roots are very delicate. Be as careful as possible during this process, as otherwise even a healthy seedling could end up becoming a weak plant.

Cloning

C loning plants is a very simple process that's been performed for ages. If you have a particularly productive plant or one with certain properties that you'd like to propagate, it's a good candidate for cloning.

To clone a plant, cut off a growing tip with no more than two leaves. This should be done during the growing phase of the plant, not during the blooming stage. Remember to only use sterile equipment to do this. Hold the cutting underwater and cut off another small piece from its stem at a 45-degree angle. This will prevent any bubbles from blocking the stem, as they could interfere with the water uptake of the cutting.

The cutting is now ready to transplant. Put it in a sponge cube and then in a seed tray. A cutting is much more sensitive than a seedling, so make sure you cater to all its needs. The growing conditions for cuttings are comparable to seedlings except for the nutrient solution, which should be at 25 percent strength.

Cuttings dry out easily because there is no root system, so ensure that they receive copious amounts of water. They usually live or die within three days. It might be a good idea to make more than one cutting and keep the strongest one.

CHAPTER

4

plant requirements

Everything that slows us down and forces patience, everything that sets us back into the slow circles of nature, is a help. Gardening is an instrument of grace.

MAY SARTON

this chapter covers plant requirements in greater depth. Some of the sections are specific to hydroponic systems, such as the nutrient solution and growing medium. Other sections cover generic concerns, such as temperature and light, and apply to plants in general.

Growing Mediums

The term *growing medium* has been mentioned several times throughout this book so far but without much detail. As you might have deduced, the growing medium essentially replaces the soil in which the plant would have otherwise grown. Soil contains a lot of minerals, organic material, living organisms, and other substances, depending on where it comes from. The soil can be chemically reactive and could potentially interact with the nutrient mixture.

To prevent any problems, hydroponic growers opt for a special growing medium that's more inert compared to soil. Note that the growing mediums used in hydroponic systems are not completely inert; they will contribute to the concentration of certain elements, such as calcium, depending on the medium used. These concentrations will in turn affect the pH levels of the nutrient solution, which is extremely important to keep in check. The sections that follow will cover the most popular growing mediums used by hydroponic gardeners and farmers. Be aware that each growing medium has different water-retention attributes, so it's a good idea to use a moisture sensor to keep track of the moisture levels of your growing medium and irrigate accordingly.

ROCKWOOL

Rockwool is a very popular growing medium. It's made of molten rock that's spun in a manner similar to cotton candy (candy floss). It's relatively inexpensive and can be purchased in large slabs with premade holes for seedlings. Rockwool strikes a good balance between water retention and oxygenation of the root system.

Unfortunately, Rockwool can't be recommended as a suitable growing medium since it poses a health risk. The fibers resemble asbestos in certain respects, and although it's less harmful than asbestos, growers must use a mask when working with it. It's also not very environmentally friendly since it doesn't degrade. Additionally, it increases the pH of the nutrient solution, so levels would need to be adjusted accordingly.

VERMICULITE

Vermiculite is a mineral that's been heated to very high temperatures, causing it to expand and form microcavities. It's very good at retaining water, but many growers complain that it tends to drown the plant, so it's not a very effective medium on its own. Better performance can be achieved by mixing vermiculite with another medium that doesn't retain water.

Unfortunately, this isn't the only downside of vermiculite. It also creates a breeding ground for bacteria, which can cause problems for your system.

In addition, vermiculite poses health problems for the workers who mine it. The mines often contain asbestos and other harmful products. In the United States, these mines are now required to conduct regular tests to ensure the vermiculite is free of asbestos. Other countries may not have these checks in place.

Vermiculite is also expensive. There are simply too many negatives to justify its use. There are much better alternatives available.

LIGHT EXPANDED CLAY AGGREGATE (LECA)

Light expanded clay aggregate, also called LECA, consists of pellets made from clay that's been heated at high temperatures until it expands. It's a porous medium that retains water very well. Overall, LECA is a suitable option for a growing medium. It's also good for mixing with other growing mediums to vary the water-retention properties with oxygen availability. The only problem with LECA is that it's not as reusable as some other options, since plant material can easily get trapped in the pores and can create a breeding ground for pathogens.

PERLITE

Perlite looks like small white rocks, but it's actually made of expanded glass pellets. Being glass, it's an inert material and perfect as a growing medium. Another bonus is that it's reasonably priced.

Perlite is reusable; you simply need to sterilize it between each crop. To do that, leave it in hot water (160–175 degrees F/70–80 degrees C) for thirty minutes.

Perlite doesn't hold water very well, so it's a good idea to mix it with another growing medium that does. If you only use perlite, you will need to irrigate very regularly to prevent the roots of your plants from drying out. If the pump fails, your crop could be at risk.

COCONUT COIR

Coconut coir is a natural growing medium with some great properties. It's essentially a waste product of the coconut industry and is therefore very inexpensive. It has excellent water-retention properties, but on its own, it could suffocate plants. Perlite is ideal to combine with coconut coir; together they form the ultimate growing medium. By adjusting the ratios of the two mediums, you can precisely cater to your crop's water-retention requirements.

Coconut coir has antifungal properties and can protect plants from particular problems, such as root rot. Another advantage is that it's reusable and can be sterilized in the same manner as perlite.

Before using coconut coir for the first time, soak it in water to get rid of any excess salt and dust particles. It's shipped in a dehydrated form, so it will expand and nearly double in size when soaked.

Light

Everybody knows that plants need light to grow, but what's not as widely known is that plants don't use the full light spectrum. They mainly use light from the visible spectrum, which has a wavelength range of 390–700µm, although they do need a small amount of ultraviolet and infrared light.

Figure 4.1 (below) shows the visible spectrum of light. It indicates the rate of photosynthesis that occurs at each wavelength. Note that very little green light is used by the plant. The green light is mostly reflected, which contributes to the plant's color.

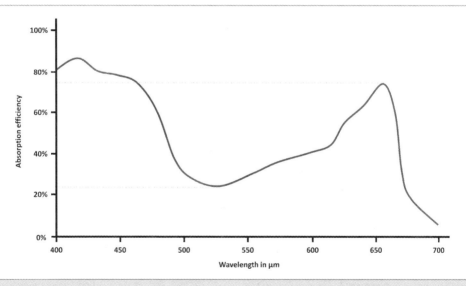

FIG. 4.1 Visible spectrum of light

Most of the photosynthesis happens at the violet, blue, orange, and red ranges. This doesn't mean that no photosynthesis happens at the other wavelengths, but it's considerably less.

If you plan to build a hydroponic system that won't be utilizing the sun as a light source, or if you intend to supplement the sun's light during the winter months, you will need to install grow lights. This is when knowledge of the most-effective wavelengths of the spectrum is essential.

The costliest aspect of running of a hydroponic system is the electricity for grow lights, so the sun should be used as a light source whenever possible. Supplementing the sun's contribution during winter months or cloudy days would only be a fraction of the cost for a system that relies exclusively on grow lights. There are several types of grow lights, but the three most popular ones are metal halide (HP), high-pressure sodium (HPS), and light-emitting diode (LED).

METAL HALIDE (HP) AND HIGH-PRESSURE SODIUM (HPS)

Metal halide is a full-spectrum light with a bias toward the blue end of the spectrum. This type of light is ideal for plants in their growing phase or for leafy green crops throughout their cycle.

High-pressure sodium is also a full-spectrum light but with a bias toward the red end of the spectrum. This type of light is ideal for plants in their flowering phase and throughout the harvest phase.

Your plants will do best if you use both types of light and switch over to the appropriate light source when they start their flowering phase. Unfortunately, these lights are quite expensive. They both require a ballast for ignition, but these ballasts are not always interchangeable, although this limitation is starting to disappear.

Some companies have begun to manufacture HPS lights with an added blue spectrum. They are a bit more costly to purchase but would result in overall savings.

HPS is better than MH in terms of efficiency; HPS produces more lumens at the same wattage. It's also better with regard to longevity. However, HPS lights steadily lose their brightness over time, so they need to be replaced well before they reach the end of their life-spans. Table 4.1 (below) illustrates the differences:

TABLE 4.1 MH versus HPS

	MH		HPS	
Watts	250W	400W	250W	400W
Lumens	14,000	20,500	26,000	45,000
Rated lifetime (h)	10,000	15,000	24,000	24,000

There are a few other disadvantages when using either of these types of lights. Both produce excess heat, which requires venting. This feature should already be built in when you purchase the light fixture. Depending on the wattage required, this would be in the form of heat-sink fins or fans.

Because of the heat they radiate, the lights need to be kept at a certain distance from the plants. Table 4.2 (below) indicates the various recommended distances based on wattage.

TABLE 4.2 Recommended distances based on wattage

WATTS	DISTANCE
250 W	12–14 inches / 30 cm–35 cm
400 W	16–24 inches / 40 cm–60 cm
1000 W	>24 inches / >60 cm

To overcome this limitation, some larger greenhouses use auto-mated, motorized rails on which the light units are constantly being moved. This allows the lights to move much closer to the plants without burning them and prevents plants from starting to grow toward a fixed light.

Another disadvantage of these types of lights is that they aren't very environmentally friendly since they contain mercury. Once again, HPS is the better option, since MH contains two to five times as much mercury.

LIGHT-EMITTING DIODE (LED)

LED grow lights are currently the most efficient choice. They are typically rated at the same wattage as their MH and HPS counterparts, so you'll notice that you get 250 W and 400 W units, but their actual consumption is much lower. For example, a 400 W LED unit will only consume 140 W, and a 250 W one consumes about 90 W. Overall, LEDs produce more light while using less energy, but what makes LED grow lights even more efficient is that they use several individual LEDs of different colors to match the wavelengths with the highest absorption rate. LED grow lights will usually emit a magenta hue, since they mostly consist of red and blue LEDs. The ratio between red and blue lights depends on the stage of the crop (growing or flowering), but they tend to be well balanced for general-purpose usage so that you don't have to switch to different LED lights for different growth periods.

The earlier versions of LED grow lights only had red and blue LEDs, but today you can get so-called full-spectrum LED grow lights. These contain a small amount of green and yellow LEDs, as well as a very small number of white, ultraviolet, and infrared LEDs. Originally, it made sense to only spend resources on the spectrum range that would contribute the highest absorption rate, but it was later discovered that plants didn't perform well under exclusively red and blue light. Certain processes can only occur at the other wavelengths, so the full spectrum requires adaptations, although to a lesser degree. Full-spectrum LED lights are a bit lighter in color and lean more toward a pink hue.

I strongly recommended that you purchase the full-spectrum LEDs instead of the ones that are red and blue only. They don't really differ in price that much, so it makes financial sense, considering the performance gain.

LED grow lights also have a few other advantages. They don't produce much heat, which means they won't burn the plants, so there aren't any proximity limitations. The light intensity of light sources drops considerably as the distance is increased, so the plant would receive more light if it's placed closer to the light source, without having to increase the wattage.

LEDs have a very long life-span, so you would spend less money on replacements. They also offer a lot of variety. For example, instead of buying the standard units of 250 W and 400 W, you could buy regular-sized individual light bulbs like the ones in your home. They come in all the socket types as well, meaning that you can simply buy some sockets that are readily available in your country and install them at any intervals that are appropriate for your grow room.

Alternatively, you can buy SMD 5050 LED strips, but currently it's nearly impossible to get full-spectrum LED strips, so red-and-blue strips are the only choice. These are not completely useless, since you can still use them to supplement your full-spectrum LEDs. For instance, if you find that your current system isn't supplying enough light, but the light sockets aren't easily movable to squeeze in more LEDs, you could add a strip or two. You could also buy a white strip, which would supplement your system with the full visible spectrum but with some waste. Another good way to make use of LED strips is to purchase red-only and blue-only strips. You can then supplement your existing supply with blue light during the growing phase and red light during the flowering phase. If you're from one of the thirty-eight countries in the world with a red, blue, and white flag and feel a bit patriotic, the combination of red, blue, and white strips might be very appealing to you.

ADDITIONAL TIPS

Regardless of the type of light source you use (natural or artificial), there are a few additional steps you can take to increase the efficiency. Most units will already come with reflectors, but if yours don't have any, consider adding them. This could increase the amount of light to the plant by 50–95 percent because the light that would otherwise be directed upward will be redirected downward in the direction of the plants.

To maximize light absorption even further, you can use some reflective material on the floor and on any other surfaces where it would make sense. For example, if you have an enclosed room, you can cover the roof, floor, and walls with reflective material. Even windows can be covered if you're not relying on the sun, or they can be covered at night with reflective blinds.

There are several reflective materials that would be appropriate for a growing area. The best one is Mylar, which is a metallic plastic sheet that is 95 percent reflective. As mentioned on page 24, you shouldn't use aluminium foil because it's quite poor at reflecting light and is better suited for reflecting heat. A practical alternative to Mylar is matte white paint, which is 75–80 percent reflective. A gloss paint doesn't perform as well.

With these improvements, you will able to stretch the effectiveness of your grow lights a bit, as well as improve on any natural light, allowing you to plant the plants closer together and use steeper A-frame inclines.

There is a limit to the amount of light that can be absorbed by a plant for photosynthesis. It peaks at around 21,500 lux but shouldn't be less than around 13,000 lux, as illustrated in figure 4.2 below.

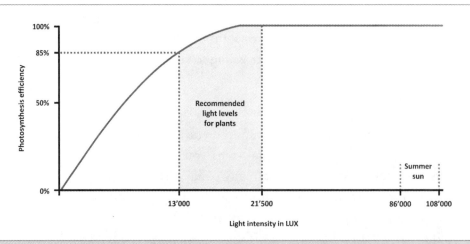

FIG. 4.2 Light absorption and efficiency

As you can see, the sun supplies four to eight times the amount of light that's required by plants. That's good news for a hydroponic grower because it means that plants can be planted closer together and stacked at steeper inclines without affecting the plants' growth.

On page 22, in the discussion about greenhouse construction, I mentioned that plants require the light from the sun but not so much of the heat (infrared spectrum). Plants also don't need as much ultraviolet (UV) light as produced by the sun, so using a heat-reflective and UV-reflective plastic sheet or glass would maximize light while dramatically limiting UV light and heat. Figure 4.3 (below) shows the spectrum of the sun.

As you can see, the greatest intensity is in the visible light spectrum, but this only accounts for 44 percent of the total energy released. About 49 percent of light is in the infrared spectrum, and 7 percent is in the UV range.

Darkness is also very important for plants. If a plant doesn't receive enough dark hours, flowers and seeds won't form correctly. Designated dark times (whether you're using natural or

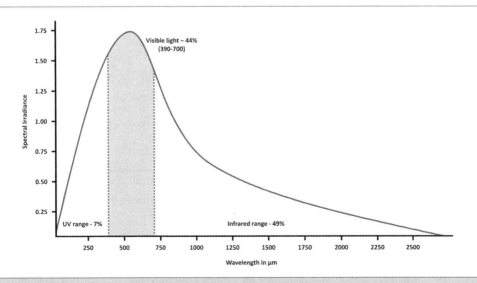

FIG. 4.3 Spectrum of the sun

artificial light) shouldn't be interrupted, as this could negatively affect the crop's development.

The ratio between light and dark hours depends on the current phase of the plant. Plants in the growing phase require between 16 and 18 hours of light. Any more than this hasn't been proven beneficial. When the plants are flowering, this can be reduced to between 10 and 14 hours of light.

The effect of the lengths of these light and dark cycles is so significant that you can force plants to bloom earlier. This technique is sometimes used to supply the flower market with enough flowers during certain peak periods, such as Valentine's Day and Mother's Day. To do this, simply switch the plant to the shorter light cycle. Depending on the type of plant, flowering can be forced as early as five weeks, but eight weeks is recommended and would produce healthier flowers. Once the flowers are harvested, the longer light cycle can be started again. This can be repeated for the lifetime of the plant.

Crops that are grown for their leaves, such as herbs, lettuce, and spinach, don't require a flowering light cycle since the intent is to have these plants remain in the growing phase perpetually. If the growing environment contains flowering plants as well, you can put the leafy crops on the shorter light cycle. The other way around isn't feasible since the shorter cycle is essential for flowering plants. If possible, you could isolate the leafy plants from the flowering plants and supply different light cycles.

Carbon Dioxide

Carbon dioxide (CO_2) is vital for plant survival, and it's the only source of carbon. It's a primary building block for plants, so you need to make sure your growing area has an ample supply. Luckily for plants, humans have gone out of their way to guarantee there's sufficient CO_2 for all plants worldwide, so if you live in a busy town or city, you will likely have more than enough already.

Concentrations decline in more remote or elevated areas, but even at diminished levels, the plants will still receive sufficient amounts to grow normally. The atmosphere contains 325–425 ppm CO_2 gas. Increasing the concentration of CO_2 available to your plants will have a very positive impact on their growth rate. By increasing the concentration to a level of 1,000–1,600 ppm, a growth gain of 50 percent or more can be achieved. But even plants have a limit to the amount of CO_2 they can tolerate. Most plants will die at concentrations above 2,000 ppm.

Note that the increased concentration range is for sustained levels. Plants can tolerate higher levels for short periods. For example, some large-scale greenhouses use CO_2 as a method of pest control. The concentration is increased up to 10,000 ppm for brief amounts of time, which is enough to kill off certain pests, such as whiteflies and spider mites, but not harm the plants. The exact optimal range varies among species, and using higher levels than required by the plant could have a negative effect on the plant's overall health, so be sure to research your crop's needs before adjusting the CO_2 levels in your grow room.

Photosynthesis (the process during which CO_2 is converted into energy and oxygen) can only occur if there is light, so if you have higher levels of CO_2, you can only leverage that advantage if you have the proper light levels. As you can see in figure 4.2 (page 46), at least 21,500 lux is needed to fully take advantage of the photosynthesis process. Photosynthesis levels tend to increase with higher temperatures (up to a certain point, of course), so maintaining a temperature in the upper range of tolerance for the crop will yield the best results. Each crop has its own needs, however, so either separate crops and move them to different greenhouses where their requirements won't conflict too much or cater to the crop with the lowest tolerance levels.

Even in a busy city, your CO_2 levels might drop considerably if there isn't enough ventilation in your growing room. Remember that CO_2 is consumed by the plants and replaced with oxygen, so you need a constant supply of normal air or air that's enriched with CO_2; otherwise, your plants' growth will suffer.

Your first option is to install an inlet fan, or install more than one if you have a large growing room. You can also install an extractor fan on the opposite side of the grow room to ensure a flow. You'll need to be able to replace the entire growing area's air in an hour, so make sure your extractor fans are sized accordingly. Install HEPA filters on your fans to filter out any dust, pollen, and other unwanted particles. Remember to clean these filters regularly and replace them when necessary.

Venting will only be able to maintain the maximum concentration that's available in the atmosphere. To go beyond this concentration level, you'll need to use CO_2 cylinders. This process is a bit more complicated and more expensive, but it could be useful if you live in an area with low atmospheric concentrations of CO_2 or if your grow space is very limited and you'd like to optimize its use.

When working in an environment that's artificially enriched with CO_2, safety is the first concern. Humans can tolerate a relatively high level of CO_2 for a very limited time, but even moderately brief exposure will have a negative impact on cognitive capabilities. A study showed that levels of 1,000 ppm for two and half hours had a significant effect on the subjects' mental faculties. If you need to work in your grow room, always vent the CO_2 while you are inside.

If you decide to go this route and are prepared to deal with the complications and higher costs, you'll need to do this correctly and automate your CO_2 supply. To do that, you'll need a CO_2 cylinder, a CO_2 sensor, a gas regulator, a gas solenoid valve (to electronically open and close the gas cylinder), a relay, and a microcontroller, such as one made by Arduino.

If you're not familiar with programming an Arduino microcontroller, search for instructional videos online. If you don't have any programming experience, get a good introductory book that specifically covers the microcontroller you are interested in.

There are also off-the-shelf systems you can purchase to maintain your CO_2 levels. These systems will control the grow area's temperature by controlling the ventilation system. It could be tricky to find a system that fits your needs perfectly, so you might need to compromise a bit. These automated systems are quite expensive and not typically appropriate for a small-scale greenhouse system at home.

The idea behind the process is to sustain an ideal CO_2 level for your crops. The sensor will monitor the CO_2 level in the growing room and open the solenoid valve when the CO_2 level falls below the ideal level. The valve is closed when those levels are reached. A regulator must be attached to the cylinder to reduce the pressure in the tank to levels suitable for the solenoid valve. If that's not done, the valve might constantly be leaking gas. The relay is just a simple switch that you can turn on and off using the microcontroller. It's ideal for when the power output of the microcontroller is not sufficient to turn the solenoid on or off directly.

When supplementing CO_2, you should have a properly sealed growing room; otherwise, you will unnecessarily vent CO_2 gas. I recommend that you use an air conditioner to regulate the grow room's temperature. If you don't choose to use an air conditioner, you will need to add a temperature sensor to the microcontroller along with another relay, which will turn on the extractor fans as soon as the temperature is too high. At the same time, you must shut off the solenoid until the temperature has dropped sufficiently. The solenoid can then be re-enabled until the CO_2 levels have been restored. If you need to ventilate your growing room regularly, it means your system is not very green, and you will be adding to the carbon footprint instead of potentially reducing it.

An important factor to consider is that the root systems of the plants don't use CO_2 and require oxygen instead. When raising the CO_2 levels, you should move your nutrient tank outside the grow room so you can properly oxygenate the water. This is critical, as otherwise the root systems might not receive a sufficient supply of oxygen. You'll still need to protect the nutrient tank from environmental elements, such as wind and rain, since they could contaminate the tank.

As you can see, supplementing CO_2 gas adds quite a few complications and caveats. However, if you want to take your hydroponic system's performance to the next level, it's something to seriously consider.

Temperature

A s discussed on page 49, plant growth can be optimized by increasing the available CO_2 and light, if the CO_2 level is maintained at the plant's saturation level and the maximum amount of light that can be absorbed is supplied. Temperature is another component that has a major influence on plant growth.

At normal atmospheric CO_2 levels, the optimal temperature for photosynthesis is 68–77 degrees F (20–25 degrees C). When CO_2 levels are increased, plants do better at higher temperatures of approximately 86–95 degrees F (30–35 degrees C). Of course, this will depend on the CO_2 tolerance level of the plant. Figure 4.4 (page 53) illustrates the interaction between temperature and CO_2 levels. Note that the photosynthesis rate drops when optimal levels of these two elements are not maintained.

At night, plants generally prefer lower temperatures of 50–68 degrees F (15–20 degrees C). The exact temperature ranges depend on the type of crop. Leafy crops, such as lettuce, prefer temperatures in the lower range, while flowering and fruit-bearing plants prefer temperatures in the higher range. Tropical plants prefer the very top of that range.

The root zone prefers a cooler environment. A temperature of about 65 degrees F (18 degrees C) is recommended because that will help minimize root rot. For every increase of 3.6 degrees F (2 degrees C) in root temperatures, the risk of root rot doubles.

The best way to control the temperature of your plants' root systems is by controlling the temperature of the nutrient solu-

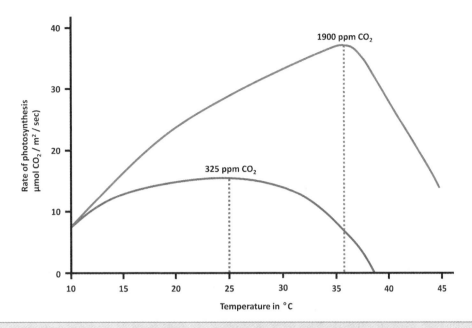

FIG. 4.4 Effects of temperature on photosynthesis

tion. A temperature range of 65–75 degrees F (18–24 degrees C) is recommended. If you know that the roots will be subjected to higher temperatures, irrigate the roots more often to cool them down.

During winter it might be necessary to raise the ambient temperature. The most efficient way to do that is to use a halogen or infrared space heater, since an air-conditioning unit consumes more electricity. Infrared heaters can even operate through glass panes, but be careful with long exposure to your eyes, as infrared light exposure could turn the clear fluid inside your eyes opaque. To control the heat you can use a mister, but this will increase the humidity, so you'll need to keep that in check. (Humidity is discussed in greater detail on page 55.)

A great way to easily control the temperature of the nutrient mix is to use a Peltier water cooling/heating block. Although a single block doesn't consume much energy, you will need to buy enough of them to heat or cool your tank by the desired number of degrees. You can easily experiment by starting with a few blocks and adding more as necessary.

Applying a current to a Peltier block will heat one side and cool the other, so you can't simply drop one of these in your tank, as doing so would have no effect. Instead, get two small aluminium or copper tanks with an input and output valve. These are generally available online or at computer shops, since they are used in water cooling for computers. Place a tank on each side of the Peltier block and use thermal paste on the surfaces where they make contact. Thermal paste is a metallic grey or white paste that conducts heat very well. It's available at most computer stores. Be careful not to use too much paste; the thermal paste should only be a very thin layer that covers the entire surface area. Depending on the size of the tanks, you should only apply one or two pea-sized beads. Ensure that there is good contact between the tanks and the Peltier block. You'll need to use some form of clamping mechanism or cable ties to secure them.

Next, connect rubber tubing to the inlets and outlets and connect a low-powered water pump to each tank. If you need to raise the temperature, turn on the Peltier block and the pump that goes to the tank on the heating side of the Peltier block. To cool the tank, use the other pump. When no pumps are running, turn off the Peltier block to save energy. This is a great little system to automate with an Arduino microcontroller. Simply connect these with relays and add a water-temperature sensor. If the temperature is too low, turn on the heating pump. If it's too high, turn on the cooling pump.

Figure 4.5 (facing page) is not to scale, since the dimensions will depend on the size of the tanks you get and the size of the Peltier unit. A small Peltier unit is 1.5 x 1.5 inches (4 x 4 cm) in size. The tanks start at 1.5 x 1.5 inches (4 x 4 cm) as well, but 1.5 x 3-inch (4 x 8-cm) and 1.5 x 4.72-inch (4 x 12-cm) sizes are also popular and will allow you to attach two or three Peltier blocks per tank. Try to minimize the distance between the Peltier system and nutrient tank as much as possible to increase efficiency.

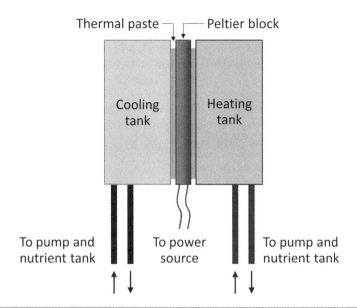

Thermal paste ⌐   ⌐ Peltier block

Cooling tank

Heating tank

To pump and nutrient tank

To power source

To pump and nutrient tank

FIG. 4.5 Using a Peltier block

Humidity

Plants prefer a humidity of 40–70 percent. If the humidity rises above this range, plants will struggle to transpire and won't be able to cool themselves. To remove excess humidity, you'll need a warmer environment that's well ventilated. This would evaporate any moisture on the leaf surfaces and vent it out of the growing area.

Failing to reduce the humidity will slow down water intake, which means a reduction in nutrient intake as well. The consequence is slower growth and possibly even death at higher levels for sustained periods.

If humidity is too low and the temperature is too high, the plants will start to lose a lot of water, which will result in an increase in water consumption. This would also increase the nutrient intake, resulting in an oversupply of certain nutrients that could lead to various crop problems. This is similar to having a nutrient solution with a concentration that's too high for the plants. To remedy this, you could add more water to the nutrient solution to dilute it a bit.

It might be difficult to maintain the correct temperature and humidity, but try to focus more on maintaining a stable level of both. Plants tend to adapt to their environment, but they won't be able to do so if there are significant fluctuations.

The root system needs to be kept at a humidity of 100 percent. This isn't difficult to accomplish with regular irrigation. Piping and nutrient containers are mostly isolated from the rest of the environment, and their high moisture conditions would contribute to an increase in humidity.

pH

The pH scale, which ranges from 0 to 14, is used to measure the acidity or alkalinity of a substance. A pH of 7 is neutral, with any number lower than that being acidic and any number above that being alkaline. Pure distilled water has a pH of 7. Plants require the pH range of the nutrient mixture to be 5.5–7.0 in order to absorb nutrients properly. This means that plants generally prefer a slightly acidic environment.

Each mineral in the nutrient mix has a different pH level at which it can be optimally absorbed. Figure 4.6 (page 57) shows the absorption efficiency for each mineral at various pH levels. Since plants have different nutrient requirements, they also have different pH preferences. Most plants will be fine with the default range, but some prefer a slightly more acidic or slightly less acidic environment. Using this chart, you can better determine the preferred pH ranges for specific plants.

When you look at figure 4.6 (facing page), you can see that a plant that requires larger amounts of iron would perform better at a pH level of 6 or below, but if it relies more on magnesium, it would need the pH to be closer to 7. The ideal pH for each plant can be calculated if the ratio of each mineral required by the plant is known.

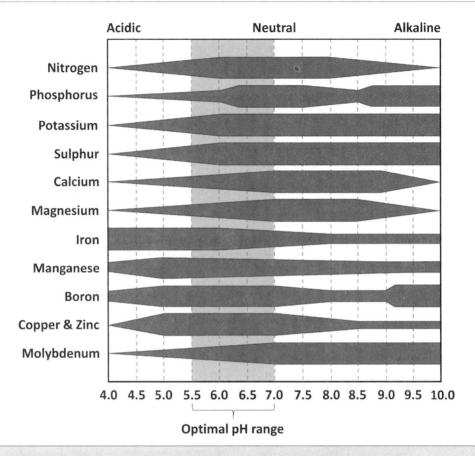

| Acidic | Neutral | Alkaline |

FIG. 4.6 Absorption efficiency for each mineral at various pH levels

The pH of the nutrient mixture can fluctuate significantly, depending on the plants' needs during the day. Therefore, you should measure the pH at regular intervals. Some people only measure it once a day, but every eight to twelve hours is preferred. If you fail to do this, the nutrient mixture might fall outside the optimal pH range for a sustained period, which would reduce the plants' ability to absorb nutrients, and growth will be affected or health issues could arise.

To measure the pH, you can either use paper pH strips or an electronic pH meter. The paper strips are not as accurate as an electronic pH meter, and they are not reusable, but they are very low cost. That said, an electronic pH meter is not very expensive either, so there's no reason not to get one.

Electronic pH meters do have a few problems of their own. Primarily, the electrode will acquire buildup over time. This will affect the reading, so the meter will have to be cleaned at least monthly. In general, pH meters need to be calibrated every month or so, as their readings will start to drift with time. When you purchase an electronic pH meter, make sure the package includes calibration liquids, directions for how to calibrate the meter, and general care instructions. Since you're going to rely heavily on this piece of equipment, take heed of these instructions.

The pH calibration liquids are simply two liquids with known pH levels, such as 4.0 and 7.0. You simply place the probe in the one of the liquids, calibrate it to that value, and then do the same with the other liquid. You will need to properly clean the probe before you insert it into either liquid to prevent cross-contamination of the liquids. These liquids need to remain as pure as possible; otherwise, you could easily calibrate your pH meter to incorrect base levels.

Unfortunately, electronic pH probes need to be replaced annually, so they will be an ongoing expense. As technology improves, these problems will eventually disappear.

Whenever you make changes to the nutrient mixture, such as adding water or adjusting nutrient concentrations, you will need to adjust the pH. This is also necessary when mixing a new batch. Before you do this, make sure the nutrient mixture has had time to dissolve and saturate properly in the water. When mixing a new batch, or if you've made significant changes, wait at least one hour to adjust the pH. During this time, use a circulation pump to ensure the nutrient mixture is constantly moving. Don't introduce a new batch to your crops before the pH has been adjusted.

You can adjust the pH of the nutrient mix by purchasing a pH kit. You will receive two liquids: one to raise the pH level and one to lower the pH level. For hydroponic systems, phosphoric acid is usually used to lower the pH, while potassium hydroxide is used to raise it. Note that these liquids are highly concentrated and only a few drops could dramatically change the pH of the nutrient mixture.

To adjust the pH level, use a dropper and only add one or two drops at a time. Use a circulation pump and allow the pH adjuster to cycle through the entire tank. You can take readings with your pH meter every few minutes and wait until the readings stabilize. If necessary, make further adjustments until the nutrient mixture is within the ideal range for your specific crop, which is generally around 6.2.

Note that it's not as simple as saying that you need five drops to adjust your pH by one point, since the adjustment depends on many factors, such as the amount of water, nutrient composition and concentration, and the type of pH adjuster being used. For example, if you have a more concentrated nutrient mixture, more pH adjuster will be required to induce the same change in a less concentrated nutrient mixture. Furthermore, the pH is logarithmic, so the further you move away from a neutral reading of 7, the more pH adjustment is needed. To avoid having to deal with all these factors, just stick to making small incremental changes until you reach the correct pH level.

You could speed up the process by recording the number of drops you added when you mixed a new batch. Then, next time, if you recreate the exact same batch, you would already know the approximate number of drops you would need to add to reach the ideal pH level. Nevertheless, you should still make sure that you get to the same pH level, so take a final reading before introducing the nutrient mix to your crops.

Note that pH drift during the day is normal, and you don't need to constantly adjust the pH levels if it has moved slightly. Focus on maintaining the 5.5–7.0 range and only adjust the pH if it falls outside this range or outside your crop's specific pH range.

Adjusting the pH can be very tedious, so I discuss on page 114 how to automate this process. It's a bit more technical and a bit more expensive to do that, but it's well worth the trouble because it would significantly reduce your day-to-day involvement.

Nutrients

P lants can't live on CO_2 and water alone, so we must supply them with the required nutrients. As I mentioned on page 27, regular fertilizers can't be used in hydroponic systems. In addition, standard fertilizers contain a lot of substances the plant doesn't use. Instead of conventional fertilizers, hydroponic farmers supply their plants with exactly the right nutrients they require and in exactly the right ratios.

Nutrient mixes are usually sold by hydroponic or gardening stores. They are premixed at generalized ratios that should be fine for most plants, so you don't really need to bother with adjusting the ratios yourself. Since some of the chemicals would interact with each other, nutrient mixes are usually sold in two or more separate bottles that you need to combine at specific ratios. The exact ratio will depend on the manufacturer, so follow their instructions closely. In some cases, only the macronutrients—also known as NPK, which stands for nitrogen (N), phosphorus (P), and potassium (K)—which comprise the bulk of the nutrients required by the plant, are included. In that case, you would have to buy a separate mixture that contains only the micronutrients.

There are at least two types of mixtures available. The first is used during the plants' growing period and contains more nitrogen. The second is used during the blooming period and contains more potassium and phosphorus. Some manufacturers offer a third mixture for the fruiting stage that contains higher potassium levels.

These premixed nutrients aren't particularly costly, so if you have easy access to them and don't want to bother with mixing your own, this is a viable option. These mixtures are highly concentrated, so a little goes a long way. Once again, the instructions on the packaging should guide you on how to mix the proper concentrations.

Table 4.3 (page 62) describes the role of all the nutrients you would typically find in a nutrient mixture, as well as their ratios.

For each nutrient, the symptoms of its deficiency (too little) or toxicity (too much) are also listed, so you can determine whether your crop is happy with the nutrient mix you're using.

Plants are quite tolerant of relatively wide nutrient ranges, but problems will pop up if there is an excess or a deficiency, so keep an eye on your crop's health and look out for the symptoms described. Check the ingredient list of commercially prepared nutrient mixtures to ensure they contain all the required nutrients. If something seems out of range, investigate why this is, since it could be that the mixture is meant for a specific range of crops or to boost crops with certain deficiencies.

Remember that if you're going to use a general-purpose nutrient mix, or even the two- or three-stage general-purpose nutrients, you won't be supplying the optimal level of nutrients required by each plant. You could still obtain decent results, but if you want to improve your yields, you will need to either purchase crop-specific nutrient mixtures (these are available for some popular crops) or learn how to mix your own.

If you decide to mix your own nutrients, table 4.4 (page 63) will provide you with a list of chemicals and quantities needed for a general-purpose mix for the growing, flowering, and fruiting stages. The amounts are listed in grams (except where noted) and will create 26 gallons (100 litres) of the nutrient mixture, depending on the concentration you need.

As noted on page 60, the chemicals can't simply be mixed in the same container, since they would interact and create insoluble compounds, rendering them useless to the plants. So two separate solutions (A and B) should be created. Based on table 4.4, this would create six bottles of nutrient solution. You can store these solutions in concentrated form using a 1.32-gallon (5-L) container for each. Only use distilled or purified water. Regular tap water is unsuitable for storing the concentrations.

The last two entries in table 4.4 are separate mixtures you need to make. These are basically A and B mixtures of micronutrients. Iron is mixed separately to prevent any interactions.

TABLE 4.3 The role and ratio of nutrients in a nutrient mixture

CHEMICAL	PPM	DESCRIPTION	DEFICIENCY	TOXICITY
Nitrogen (N)	100–450	Macro NPK nutrient responsible for producing chlorophyll. Important during the growth period. Uptake is higher in light periods.	Causes spindly plants with small yellow leaves. Some plant parts may turn purple.	Overly vigorous growth, dark green leaves, delayed fruit ripening, more susceptible to pests.
Phosphorus (P)	10–100	Macro NPK nutrient responsible for producing sugars, adenosine triphosphate (ATP), fruit/flowers, and root growth. More important during the flowering period. Uptake is higher in lower-light periods.	Stunted growth and dark green color. Lower leaves become yellow and may tint purple. Leaves curl and droop. Fruit and root production are compromised.	Reduction in copper and zinc availability.
Potassium (K)	100–650	Macro NPK nutrient responsible for protein synthesis, hardiness, root growth, and sugar and starch production. Uptake is higher in lower-light periods.	Growth slows and leaves develop mottling. The plant becomes prone to fungus.	May cause magnesium deficiency.
Calcium (Ca)	70–300	Macronutrient responsible for cell formation and new roots.	Stunts growth and causes crinkled leaves. Shoots die and flowers fall. Tomatoes will develop brown spots on their bottoms, called blossom-end rot.	May cause magnesium deficiency.
Sulphur (S)	20–250	Macronutrient responsible for protein synthesis, water uptake, fruiting, and seeding. A natural fungicide.	Rare, but turns young leaves yellow with purple bases.	Slows growth. Causes small leaves.
Magnesium (Mg)	10–95	Needed for chlorophyll production.	Older leaves curl. Causes yellowing between veins. Only new leaves will be green.	Rare
Iron (Fe)	0.5–6	Needed for chlorophyll production and respiration of sugars for energy.	New growth is pale and flowers drop. Causes yellowing between veins, and edges may die.	Difficult to spot, but rare.

Boron (B)	0.1–0.8	Needed for cell formation.	Causes brittle stems and poor growth. Stems twist and split.	Leaf tips turn yellow and die off.
Manganese (Mn)	0.3–4	Helps growth and oxygen formation during photosynthesis.	Causes yellowing between veins and failure to bloom.	Reduces iron availability.
Zinc (Zn)	0.1–0.5	Needed for chlorophyll production, respiration and nitrogen metabolism.	Small leaves. Causes crinkled edges.	Reduces iron availability.
Molybdenum (Mo)	0.02–0.07	Needed for nitrogen metabolism.	Small yellow leaves.	Could turn tomato leaves bright yellow, but rarely.
Copper (Cu)	0.05–0.1	Needed for photosynthesis and respiration.	Causes pale, yellow-spotted leaves.	Reduces iron availability.
Cobalt (Co)	0.01–0.05	Not typically in nutrient mixes. Helps legumes with nitrogen uptake. Improves seeds' drought resistance.	Causes reduced nitrogen uptake in legumes and struggling seed germination during drought.	Causes iron deficiency. Loss of leaves, pale leaves, and veins.
Chloride (Cl-)	15–20	Not typically in nutrient mixes. Aids plant growth and is required for photosynthesis.	Causes blotchy pale leaf areas or dying regions.	Smaller leaves with dying edges.
Nickel (Ni)	1–20	Not typically in nutrient mixes. Helps with nitrogen uptake and seed germination.	Causes discoloration of leaves. Seeds from deficient plants often fail to germinate.	Causes iron deficiency. Inhibits seed germination and root growth. Causes deformed flowers and impedes photosynthesis.

TABLE 4.4 A general-purpose mix for the growing, flowering, and fruiting stages

CHEMICAL	GROW	BLOOM	FRUIT	SOLUTION
Calcium nitrate – $Ca(NO_3)_2$	158.73	108.47	211.64	A
Potassium nitrate – KNO_3	55.29	74.07	74.07	A
Sulphate of potash – K_2SO_4	12.17	12.17	44.97	B
Monopotassium phosphate – KH_2PO_4	36.77	36.77	36.77	B
Magnesium sulphate Heptahydrate – $MgSO_4·7H_2O$	64.02	63.49	63.49	B
Concentrated Trace Mix	2 tsp/10 ml	2 tsp/10 ml	2 tsp/10 ml	B
Concentrated Iron Mix	3.38 oz/100 ml	3.38 oz/100 ml	3.38 oz/100 ml	A

Tables 4.5 and 4.6 (below) show the amounts for these mixtures. They must be mixed at a 1:5 ratio compared to the nutrient concentration mixes in table 4.4, so this means they must be mixed in a 1-quart (1-L) container. Once again, do not use tap water when you make these concentrates.

TABLE 4.5 Concentrated trace mix

CHEMICAL	GRAMS
Zinc sulphate (ZnSO$_4$)	2.2
Manganese sulphate (MnSO$_4$)	15.4
Copper sulphate (CuSO$_4$)	0.8
Boric acid (H3BO$_3$)	28.6
Sodium molybdate (Na$_2$MoO$_4$)	0.25

TABLE 4.6 Concentrated iron mix

CHEMICAL	GRAMS
Chelated iron (FeEDTA)	19.48

When mixing these concentrates, first fill the bottle with 80 percent of the purified water required for the mixture. For the macro mixes, it would be 1 gallon (4 L) of water and about 27 ounces (800 ml) for the micro mix. This doesn't have to be exact because it will be topped up afterward; it's just to leave you some room while mixing.

Dissolve each ingredient separately before adding the next one, and make sure that it dissolves completely. Don't add all ingredients at the same time. No sediment should be visible near the bottom. Dissolve it by simply closing the bottle and shaking it vigorously.

Top up each of the bottles with additional purified water until it's filled; it is then ready to be used in your nutrient tanks. You will only add a relatively small amount of these concentrations to prepare a nutrient tank for your crops. The exact concentration will depend on the crop. (Table 5.1, page 76, lists the concentrations preferred by various popular crops.)

Getting hold of the macro ingredients could be easier, so if you struggle with the micro ingredients, try to find a premixed mixture online. Since you need a smaller quantity of the micro mixture, the shipping costs should be nominal or even be free.

Mixing your own nutrient mix will most likely save you a bit of money, but even more important, it will give you a starting point to adjust your nutrient mix and tailor it to each crop. Unfortunately, this is quite a complicated process. There currently is no easy and affordable way to monitor the consumption of individual elements of your crop. If you could, you would know when to top up the nutrient tank with the exact chemicals required as they are depleted from the nutrient mixture.

The problem is that each plant type requires a different nutrient mixture, but even more complicated is the fact that nutrient needs fluctuate significantly depending on the plant's life stage (seedling versus adult) or crop cycle (growing, flowering, fruiting). A lab can perform an analysis for you, but this could be prohibitively expensive. Still, you would only need to do this once for a specific crop type, so if you know you're going to farm lettuce on a commercial scale, the costs could be worth it.

For a home grower, this won't make financial sense, but there are other ways you can figure out the optimal nutrient solution for a specific crop. You could run several parallel experiments with various mixtures and monitor the effect of each.

To set up your experiment, you will need to exclude as many variables as possible. Find a healthy plant specimen and clone it multiple times. This will be the only plant you'll use until your experiment has been concluded; otherwise, individual plant variations will come into play and skew your results. Furthermore, your environmental conditions must be the same for each plant. This means uniform light, temperature, humidity, watering cycles, initial water quality, pH, the concentration of nutrients, and the growing medium. The fewer factors that vary, the more accurate your results will be. Don't forget that you must dilute the nutrient mixture down to 25 percent for cuttings.

Next, start growing your cuttings at the same time, with the only variable in the system being the composition of the nutrient mixture. Each nutrient mixture should only have a single chemical changed over a wide spectrum. For example, from the generic mixture provided in table 4.4 (page 68), calcium nitrate is at 158.73 g for the growing-stage formulation. So have one nutrient tank at this level, another at maybe 5 percent higher (166.67 g), and another one at 5 percent lower (150.79 g). Add tanks for each 5 percent interval in both directions, up to 100 percent. This should give you the original plus 40 tanks. Note that the tanks could be quite small, so you don't need to have a huge space to run these experiments.

Run the experiment for one to three weeks (depending on the crop), until the cuttings become established small plants with well-developed root systems. This will determine the optimal nutrient level of that one chemical. Repeat the experiment for each chemical. Once you find the optimal nutrient solution to get your cuttings growing into healthy small plants, record this as the optimal nutrient solution for cuttings of that type of crop.

The experiment should be restarted with fresh cuttings using this optimal nutrient solution. You can then start with new experimental nutrient solutions when the cuttings have become small plants with developed root systems. This must be a defined period, such as two weeks. You can then establish the optimal nutrient mixture for when the crops are small plants.

This is repeated as many times as necessary until you have covered all the identifiable stages of the plant. The exact stages are determined by the specific crop and are usually obvious to see. For more ambiguous crops, do some research online to help you identify them.

Performing these experiments is very tedious, and it could take years to find the optimal levels for several crops. Therefore, it's best to have a greenhouse in which you use the best nutrient mixture you're currently aware of for each crop and run your experiments separately. Don't run your experiments in a greenhouse, however, because you can't control the exact amount of sunlight you'll get each day. Instead, run them inside a darkened room where you can fully control the light cycle using artificial light. This way, you can start to produce crops immediately with what you have and apply your breakthroughs from your experiments as you discover them. The room doesn't have to be very big since you can stack multiple growing trays vertically, each with its own grow lights.

Discovering these little breakthroughs can be very satisfying, even if they result in something as simple as a 5 percent greater yield. These breakthroughs stack up, and in time you could master a vast number of crops.

It would be great to share this knowledge with your fellow growers to eliminate any duplicate experiments. If you have a few friends who also have hydroponic systems, get each one to find the optimal nutrient levels of just one crop at a time and share the results with everybody.

You can also join online discussion forums where you can find growers who already have found optimum values for some crops, or you can get others to join you in running these experiments, regardless of where each person is located. Doing this will widen your network and provide you with faster results.

5

nutrient tank

Remember that children, marriages, and flower gardens reflect the kind of care they get.

H. JACKSON BROWN JR.

this chapter delves into more detail on how to mix a new batch of nutrients, how to maintain the mixture, and how to deal with any potential problems. The first step is to get the right size nutrient tank. If the tank is too small, you will need to constantly add new nutrients, raise the water level, and adjust the pH level. If the tank is too large and something goes wrong with a batch that requires you to flush it and start from scratch, you will waste a lot of water and nutrients. A good rule of thumb is to go for 20–27 ounces (600–800 ml) per plant.

Algae can clog the system and will consume the nutrients in the tank, leaving your crops undernourished. Therefore, the water in the nutrient tank should not be exposed to any light because this could cause algae to grow in the system. This is true for any location in your system, so always use dark pipes and tubes and use a lid or cover for your nutrient tank.

Water Pump

Depending on the system you're using, you will likely need a water pump to push the nutrients through it. Purchase a pump that's appropriate for your setup. An important consideration is the height at which it can pump water. You don't need a pump that's overly strong, since you only need it to provide a decent spray intensity via the nozzles or a slow trickle if you're not using spray nozzles in your system.

A good choice is a pump with multiple speeds so you can simply select the speed that's best suited for your system. A multispeed pump will also allow you to make changes to your system if you need to.

Since the water pump is vital to your crop's survival, it's a good idea to buy a backup one, since these pumps can fail without warning. If you have multiple nutrient tanks, you might want to buy two or more backup pumps.

Oxygenating the Water

I n addition to a water pump, you'll also need to oxygenate the water. There are two options for doing this. The first is to use an aquarium air pump with an air stone. You'll need a relatively strong air pump, since it must be powerful enough to properly disrupt the water's surface. Note that the air stone could clog with time, so you will need to clean it or buy a new one when you notice a decline in performance. Just like the water pump, the air pump could also fail at any time, so you should buy a backup. The air pump is especially vital for the water culture system (see page 15).

The second method for oxygenating the water involves attaching a T connector to the outgoing irrigation line and allowing some of the water to fall back into the tank from a height. This will cause disruption of the water's surface and help oxygenate the water. You could also just use a weak second pump. Pumps are affordable, and you don't need to reduce the pressure of your irrigation line. If you don't use a secondary pump, make sure that the fallback line is thinner than the irrigation line to ensure that most of the pressure is still used for irrigation. If you recycle the water back into the nutrient tank, add a filter to capture any debris and clean it regularly to prevent it from clogging.

You will also need to add small fans to the nutrient tank to allow fresh air to cycle through the tank area. This will prevent mildew from forming. A small 12V DC fan on each side is sufficient. One fan should direct air into the tank, and the other fan should direct it outward. These fans are typically used in computers, so a computer store would likely stock them.

Treating the Water

I t's possible to use tap water for hydroponic systems, provided it's potable and not too hard. Water hardness is an indication of a number of soluble substances and other impurities that are present in the water.

It's a good idea to treat the water before using it. To kill off any living organisms, you can treat it with chlorine. Add ¼ teaspoon (1 ml) of chlorine for every 2 quarts (2 L) of water. Let the water rest under a UV lamp for twenty-four hours. The UV light will help break down the chlorine and assist with purification.

A UV light is a great way to destroy any living organisms in the water. However, don't add a UV light to the nutrient tank when nutrients are present because it will cause some nutrients to become insoluble and useless to the plants.

You can also use water that has been filtered using reverse osmosis (RO), but this could add significant costs to the entire system. RO filters need to be replaced quite regularly, and they can be expensive, depending on where you get them.

Nutrient Mixtures and Related Concerns

O nce the water has been processed, you can start to add the nutrients. Before doing that, though, you will need to determine the current number of dissolved solids in the water. Pure distilled water doesn't have any dissolved solids, but tap water will contain some traces due to the water-treatment process.

To measure dissolved solids, you'll need an electro-conductivity (EC) meter. This is sometimes referred to as a TDS (total dissolved solids) meter, but it returns a different unit of measure.

A popular and easy-to-understand unit of measure for TDS is parts per million (ppm). This simply means how many milligrams of dissolved solids are present in 1 quart (1 L) of water. A milligram is one millionth of a kilogram, or 1 ppm. Another unit of measure is EC, which is an indication of how conductive the liquid is. The higher the reading, the more dissolved solids are present. EC is expressed as mS/cm, and 1 mS/cm is the equivalent of 700 ppm. The final unit of measure is conducting factor (CF). A CF reading of 10 is simply 1 mS/cm, or 700 ppm.

EC/TDS meters need to be recalibrated at least once a year. Ensure that you also properly clean the meter to prevent any buildup on the electrodes. Be careful not to bend the electrodes even the tiniest bit because this could influence the reading. If it looks like the electrodes could bend easily, simply rinse them rather than making any direct contact with them.

Measure your treated water to determine its TDS. A reading above 200 ppm is not good news and means that you will need to use an RO filter to reduce its TDS. That's because those dissolved solids aren't usable to the plant. Since each crop can only tolerate a certain maximum TDS level, the undissolved solids will reduce the number of nutrients available to the plant.

If you are supplying different types of crops from the same nutrient tank (even though this is not recommended), use a nutrient concentration that is slightly higher than the crop that requires the lowest nutrient concentration. If you don't, that crop won't be able to take up any nutrients. If your water is within the recommended limits, you can start to add the nutrients to the tank until you have the preferred TDS level for your specific crop.

Add the nutrients from the A and B concentrates one at a time, and dissolve them completely before adding the next. This will prevent any flaking that could result if the chemicals from the two bottles should interact, as that will leave those chemicals in an insoluble state and useless to the plants. This is the reason for storing them in separate bottles in the first place.

Note that temperature can affect your EC/TDS readings. Most probes will have a temperature sensor as well and will compensate for this. Temperature also influences the plant's TDS requirements. The plant will require a higher TDS in colder temperatures and a lower TDS in warmer temperatures, since the plant will consume more water to allow it to transpire.

You will need to monitor your crop to check for water-based problems, such as *Pythium* (root rot). This and other bacteria can be controlled by adding beneficial bacteria to your nutrient tank. You can purchase these from certain hydroponic stores.

An alternative to adding beneficial bacteria is to add very small amounts of chlorine or hydrogen peroxide to the tank at specific intervals. Note that this should never be used in combination with beneficial bacteria, since all microbes would be killed.

Hydrogen peroxide is preferred over chlorine because it's not as harsh and will simply break down into water and oxygen. It can also help plants absorb nutrients better. Note that too much of either could start to brown the roots, so watch for this carefully. Add ½ teaspoon (3 ml) of hydrogen peroxide for every 1.85 gallons (7 L) of water. Buy a 35 percent diluted hydrogen peroxide solution or adapt the ratios accordingly.

The nutrient tank should be flushed and its contents replaced every time a new crop is planted or if a new crop cycle starts. If you use a separate nutrient mixture for growth, flowering, and fruiting, you will need to replace the solution at each of these stages. If any of these cycles are quite long, you will need to replace it every week or two, depending on the crops. A good indicator for when to replace the solution is after you have topped up the entire contents of the tank one time. This means that the plants have consumed one full nutrient tank of water and nutrients.

There are a few reasons why the nutrient solution needs to be replaced regularly. The first is to control the pathogens, since you will be flushing the nutrient solution completely and cleaning out the nutrient tank before adding a fresh, sterilized batch of water with nutrients. This isn't essential if you control your nutrient solution well with hydrogen peroxide and eliminate all light from entering the system.

The second reason is that despite your best efforts, the nutrient mix will not be perfect for each crop because crop needs could fluctuate and cause imbalances in the ratios of the chemicals. This could result in deficiencies of some chemicals and an excess of others. Unfortunately, EC/TDS meters only measure the overall nutrient concentration. Although you could use a lab to test the concentration and then adjust your nutrient mixture accordingly, that would be much more expensive than just replacing the tank and starting with a new batch.

If you don't want to simply dump the nutrient solution, the easiest alternative is to use it for watering your houseplants, soil-based garden plants, or lawn. This might not be legal, depending on your locale, since it could be considered contamination of the soil, especially if you live near a river or dam.

You could try reverse osmosis to recover the water, but the chemicals won't be usable. This is a good option if you live in an area where water is very scarce, but the cost of the filters could be a limiting factor.

A more complicated method to reduce waste is to allow the crop to use most of the nutrient tank by not always topping it up to 100 percent. The TDS needs to be monitored regularly. Water is only added if the TDS reading is too high and only the correct amount of water is added to bring it back in check. Nutrients are also added if the TDS reading is too low. When the tank reaches a water level of 20 percent, or possibly 10 percent if you have a very large tank, you can then flush the system and start with a new batch.

Increase the nutrient concentration evenly as the water level drops, but do so only marginally. You could push the concentration by 10–20 percent. For example, if you opt for a 15 percent increase, your solution would be at 100 percent strength when the water level is at 100 percent, 107.5 percent when the water level is at 60 percent, and 115 percent when the water level is at 20 percent. You can do the same with your irrigation frequency by also increasing it by 10–20 percent. All of this is done to try to increase the number of useful nutrients to the plants when the nutrient solution becomes saturated with excess, unusable concentrations of some of the chemicals. If you see any signs of toxification, reduce the concentration a bit.

As your nutrient tank depletes, it will become more sensitive to fluctuations in pH as well as concentration, and you will need to make more frequent adjustments. The more aspects you automate, the less labor-intensive this process will be.

Crop Information

The pH and TDS levels of popular crops are shown in table 5.1 (below). Several sources have been used to assemble this data, so averages have been used when the sources are not in agreement and in some cases the ranges have been expanded.

TABLE 5.1 The pH and TDS levels of popular crops

CROP	PH	PPM/TDS	CROP	PH	PPM/TDS
Artichokes	6.5-7.5	560-1,260	Eggplants	6.0	1,200-2,450
Asparagus	6.0-6.8	980-1,260	Endive, Chicory, and Radicchio	5.5	1,100-1,680
Banana	5.5-6.5	1,260-1,540	Garlic	6.0-6.5	980-1,260
Basil	5.5-6.5	700-1,120	Leeks	6.5-7.0	980-1,260
Beans	6.0-6.5	1,400-2,800	Lettuce	6.0-7.0	560-840
Beetroots	6.0-6.5	1,260-3,500	Marjoram	6.9	1,120-1,400
Blackcurrant	6.0	980-1,260	Melons	5.5-6.0	1,400-1,750
Blueberries	4.0 -5.0	1,260-1,400	Mint	5.5-6.5	1,400-1,680
Bok Choy (Pak-choi)	7.0	1,050-1,400	Okra	6.5	1,400-1,680
Broad Bean	6.0-6.5	1,260-1,540	Onions	6.0-7.0	980-1,260
Broccoli	6.0-6.8	1,900-2,450	Oregano	6.0-7.0	1,120-1,400
Brussels Sprouts	6.5-7.5	1,750-2,100	Parsley	5.5-7.0	560-1,260
Cabbages	6.5-7.5	1,750-2,100	Parsnips	6.0	980-1,260
Carrots	5.8-6.4	1,120-1,400	Passion Fruit	6.5	840-1,680
Cauliflower	6.0-7.0	1,050-1,400	Pawpaws	6.5	1,400-1,680
Celery	6.5	1,260-1,680	Peas (Snow and Snap)	6.0-7.0	980-1,260
Chiles	6.0-6.5	1,260-1,540	Pepino	6.0-6.5	1,400-3,500
Chives	6.0-6.5	840-1,540	Peppers	5.8-6.3	1,400-2,100
Cucumbers	5.5-6.0	1,100-1,750			

CROP	PH	PPM/TDS
Peppers, Bell	6.0–6.5	1,400–1,750
Peppers, Chiles	5.5–6.0	300–500
Pineapples	5.0–6.0	1,400–1,680
Potatoes	5.0–6.0	1,400–1,750
Pumpkins	5.0–7.0	1,260–1,680
Radishes	6.0–7.0	840–1,540
Red Currants	6.0	980–1,260
Rhubarb	5.0–6.0	840–1,400
Rosemary	5.5–6.0	700–1,120
Sage	5.5–6.5	700–1,120
Scallions (Green Onions)	6.0–7.0	980–1,260
Silver Beets	6.0–7.0	1,260–1,610
Spinach	5.5–7.0	1,260–1,610

CROP	PH	PPM/TDS
Strawberries	5.5–6.5	1,260–1,540
Summer Squash (Marrow)	6.0	1,260–1,680
Sweet Corn	6.0	840–1,680
Sweet Potatoes	5.5–6.0	1,400–1,750
Swiss Chard	6.0–7.0	1,260–1,610
Taro	5.0–5.5	1,750–2,100
Thyme	5.5–7.0	560–1,120
Tomatoes	5.5–6.5	1,400–3,500
Turnips	6.0–6.5	1,260–1,680
Watermelons	5.8	1,260–1,680
Winter Squash	5.5–7.5	1,260–1,680
Zucchini	6.0	1,260–1,680

CHAPTER

6

automation

The garden suggests there might be a place
where we can meet nature halfway.

MICHAEL POLLAN

if you got this far, you should now be able to set up your own greenhouse and run a successful hydroponic system. If you have enough time to tend to it a few times a day, you don't even need to look at automating anything. Even if you have a demanding day job, you will likely still have enough time to manage your greenhouse twice a day or so.

Before you delve into automating your setup, you might want to give it a trial run and see what the system demands from you. Doing that will help you identify the tasks you dislike so you'll know which areas you might want to automate.

The beauty of hydroponics is that you can automate almost everything. The only tasks that are a bit difficult to automate are those that would require a robotic arm, such as planting seeds, removing old crops, removing dead leaves, pruning, and harvesting. While it's not impossible to automate these tasks, explaining how to do so is beyond the scope of this book.

The Basics

If you think about it, most entry-level hydroponic systems already cover some automation. Water is automatically oxygenated via an air pump, and irrigation is handled by a water pump. If you used a growing medium that doesn't hold water, or if you're using an aeroponic system, your water pump will run constantly. Even the drip system can be run constantly at a trickle.

For ebb and flow, a simple timer unit is used to control the flooding and draining periods. A timer unit is also useful for when you're working with a growing medium that can hold water. If you're using artificial lights, these would be placed on a timer as well.

This covers most aspects of hydroponics, so with nothing more than a water pump, air pump, timers, and lights, you would only need to tend to your system about twice a day to deal with the manual processes. Overall, it should take you an hour or less a day, depending on the size of your growing area.

For most people, this is sufficient, so if you fall into this category, you could close this book now and kick off your hydroponics project, if you haven't done so already. But if you want some additional automation, keep reading.

The rest of this book will identify the various areas that can benefit from automation and how you can best accomplish that. You can either implement these selectively or build the ultimate system that basically only requires you to plant the seeds, tend to some pruning, and wait until harvest.

Commercial Equipment

There are several commercial units that can be used to automate particular tasks within a hydroponic system. Some units simply log various information, such as air temperature, water temperature, humidity, pH, and EC. Their functionality varies greatly, so do some research to find out which type of unit would be the most beneficial and cost-effective for your needs.

More expensive units can automatically turn air conditioners on and off and can also control extractor fans. Adding one of these would go a long way in controlling the environmental conditions of your growing area, which could save your crops on unexpectedly warm or cold days when you aren't around to manage the situation directly.

Unit types range from doing one specific function, such as controlling humidity levels, to all-in-one units that can handle most of the tasks for you. These controllers typically are designed to be used in much larger greenhouses for commercial farming. They tend to deal with higher water pressures and have more durable connectors and waterproof buttons. They also include fail-safe features.

If you intend to do large-scale commercial hydroponic farming, take a look at the devices available. It can be a bit tricky to find the right type of equipment that's compatible with other equipment. Buying an all-in-one unit resolves that problem, but it also creates a single point of failure. Repair time could result in a loss of crops unless you have a backup unit, which would double your costs. Buying individual systems could cost a bit more in total, but replacing individual units is much less expensive.

If you are a home grower or only have a small greenhouse, even if it's for commercial purposes, you might be disappointed when you see the prices of these units. Most units cost between a few hundred dollars and up to a few thousand dollars. The average cost of a unit could end up being more than the cost of building a small greenhouse and the hydroponic system combined. The reason for the high price is that these units are not mass-produced and are considered speciality commercial/industrial equipment. If hydroponics ever becomes mainstream, the cost would likely drop considerably.

Hydroponics Crop Manager Kit

For the home-based grower, DIY automation is the only viable option. Unfortunately, the learning curve can be quite steep and many people find it too daunting. Plus, you would need to learn (or already have) some basic electronics and programming skills.

Tinkering can be quite exciting and fascinating, but if that isn't your forte, my Hydroponics Crop Manager Kit (hydroponicscropmanager.com) might interest you. This is basically a paint-by-numbers version of DIY automation. The heart of the kit is the software, which can be purchased on its own. The hardware can be ordered separately from popular sites such as amazon.com, ebay.com, and aliexpress.com, and you only need to order the parts you are interested in. The purpose of this kit is to eventually automate every aspect of home-based or commercial hydroponic farming.

The Hydroponics Crop Manager Kit makes use of the Raspberry Pi and Arduino microcontroller boards. These are essentially small programmable computers on which the Hydroponics Crop Manager software runs. With the kit, you don't need to worry about understanding how to program these microcontroller boards, and if you include the microcontrollers in your order, the software will come pre-installed, so you can simply power up the system and start using it.

Once configured, the system will connect to your Wi-Fi network, and you can access it as a normal website using your browser. The system allows you to set up your greenhouse layout and the crops you have. It can be scaled quite easily and can manage multiple hydroponic systems via the same interface.

You basically just need to tell the software what types of crops you have and how to care for them. Next, you'll need to tell it what kind of hardware you have. It will only be able to care for your crops to the extent that it has the hardware to do so. For example, if you only have a temperature sensor, and you inform the sensor that your crop prefers a certain temperature range, it will only be able to monitor the temperature and inform you if it's too high or too low, but it won't be able to do anything about it. If you have a relay switch that can turn on an air conditioner or two relays that can turn on fans or a heater, the system would be able to detect and control the temperature of your growing area. The software will also log all the data from the various sensors, so you can monitor your system's health, day-to-day environmental conditions, nutrient consumption, pH levels, and so on.

A more advanced feature is the ability to manage your nutrient solution. With the correct hardware, you can automatically adjust the pH and nutrient concentrations. It will also manage hydroperoxide administration, pH sensor calibration, EC sensor calibration, and the flushing, sterilization, and refilling of nutrient tanks. Based on the crop, it can create a new batch of nutrients and switch it out, depending on the crop's stage.

The Hydroponics Crop Manager Kit is a cost-effective option if you're not interested in building and programming these automation systems yourself. It also provides you with a good base platform on which you can add your own customized options.

When I started out in the field of hydroponics, it was clear that I and other growers could benefit considerably from automating the process as much as possible. But when I did some research, I discovered that the available automation was limited, fragmented, and very expensive. Consequently, the idea for the Hydroponics Crop Manager was born. The intent of the system is to offer growers an affordable platform to add automation to their hydroponic systems without having to acquire a wide variety of skills. Nevertheless, have a look at what other systems are available and decide for yourself which options are best for your needs. Some systems are meant for different scales, so compare their costs and capabilities with other commercial systems and choose the one that is the most appropriate for your setup.

DIY Automation

I f you prefer to get your hands dirty and have some technical skills, this section will point you in the right direction. In "The Basics" (page 80), I discussed the entry-level DIY automation that you can apply from day one. Now I'll go into much greater detail on how to automate specific tasks and monitor your environment and your system's health.

For many small growers, this might seem too daunting, but it doesn't necessarily have to be. You'll need to learn some basic electronics, but 99 percent of the work has already been done by others. Exact instructions for how to build these hydroponic units are readily available online. Most of the sensors will come preassembled, so you don't need to worry about soldering and working with base electronic components (for the most part, at least).

MICROCONTROLLERS

Automation beyond the basics requires a programmable microcontroller board. There are several of these available, but the most popular two are the Arduino series of boards and Raspberry Pi boards.

The Raspberry Pi is the more powerful board. It has much more processing power and working memory (RAM) and can run much larger and more complex applications. These boards are also much more expensive and use more electricity, so you would need a larger battery backup system.

For a basic home operation, a Raspberry Pi board might be overkill, unless you want to run a more complex application on it that allows you to configure and interact with your system and view logs and reports. Even for basic interaction, such as configuration, an Arduino will likely still suffice.

The Raspberry Pi comes with several built-in features. The feature list below is based on the Raspberry Pi 3:

- 1.2GHz, 64-bit quad-core ARM CPU
- VideoCore 4 GPU
- 802.11n Wi-Fi
- Bluetooth V4.1
- 1GB RAM
- 4 USB ports
- HDMI port
- Ethernet port
- 3.5mm audio jack / composite video
- Camera interface
- Display interface
- Micro SD card slot
- 40 general-purpose IO pins

General-purpose IO pins are where you will connect your sensors. Some sensor pins must be connected to specific pins in this array, but you can usually move them to other pins.

The pins on the Raspberry Pi can be used for input and output, but they are digital, so you can't read or write an analog signal. This is quite annoying since many sensors return an analog signal. The best solution to this problem is to get a digital-to-analog add-on board. Another option is to run all your complex and resource-intensive code on the Raspberry Pi but use an Arduino to connect to the sensors.

Arduinos usually have several digital pins and a few analog pins. This helps simplify the interaction with the sensors. Another advantage is that you can get several Arduino boards with different capabilities, and they are usually very inexpensive. One of the most popular ones is the Arduino Nano, and it's the least-expensive one as well. The Arduino Nano only has a fraction of the processing power of the Raspberry Pi, and its RAM and onboard flash memory (where applications are stored) is very limited. Still, it has a very small footprint and uses very little power. Even with its limitations, it is the ideal controller for a hydroponic system.

Table 6.1 (facing page) lists all the Arduino controllers currently available and how they differ.

You can see from table 6.1 that all except one of these controllers have very low specifications. Programming these devices can be tricky when dealing with the small amounts of RAM available, and you'll need to think about how you can optimize your code, which is good practice regardless.

Some of these boards could be a bit difficult to find, and others might be more expensive than better or more popular boards, so before you make any decisions, explore what is available to you. Online stores are the best places for these boards, including sensors. The Nano and Mini boards are quite popular and ideal for a smaller number of sensors. If you want to go larger, the Mega will probably be your best choice.

TABLE 6.1 Comparison of Arduino controllers

NAME	CPU	ANALOG IO	DIGITAL IO	ROM (KB)	RAM (KB)	FLASH (KB)
101	32 MHz	6/0	14/4	--	24	196
Gemma	8 MHz	1/0	3/2	0.5	0.5	8
LilyPad	8 MHz	6/0	14/6	0.5	1	16
LilyPad SimpleSnap	8 MHz	4/0	9/4	1	2	32
LilyPad USB	8 MHz	4/0	9/4	1	2.5	32
Mega 2560	16 MHz	16/0	54/15	4	8	256
Micro	16 MHz	12/0	20/7	1	2.5	32
MKR1000	48 MHz	7/1	8/4	--	32	256
Pro ATmega168	8 MHz	6/0	14/6	0.5	1	16
Pro ATmega328P	16 MHz	6/0	14/6	1	2	32
Pro Mini 8MHz	8 MHz	6/0	14/6	1	2	32
Pro Mini 16MHz	16 MHz	6/0	14/6	1	2	32
Uno	16 MHz	6/0	14/6	1	2	32
Zero	48 MHz	6/1	14/10	--	32	256
Due	84 MHz	12/2	54/12	--	96	512
Esplora	16 MHz	--	--	1	2.5	32
Ethernet	16 MHz	6/0	14/4	1	2	32
Leonardo	16 MHz	12/0	20/7	1	2.5	32
Mega ADK	16 MHz	16/0	54/15	4	8	256
Mini	16 MHz	8/0	14/6	1	2	32
Nano ATmega168	16 MHz	8/0	14/6	0.5	1	16
Nano ATmega328P	16 MHz	8/0	14/6	1	2	32
Yùn ATmega32U4	16 MHz	12/0	20/7	1	2.5	32
Yùn AR9331	400 MHz	12/0	20/7	1	16MB	64MB
Arduino Robot	16 MHz	6/0	20/6	1	2.5	32
MKRZero	48 MHz	7/1	22/12	--	32	256

Note that there are several ways to connect multiple Arduino boards, so you could set up a network of these to automate your growing area. Similar connectivity is available for the Raspberry Pi as well, which means that it can be joined in the network if required.

The most popular way to connect to sensors, components, and other controller boards is via a digital or analog pin, UART serial connection, serial peripheral interface (SPI), or inter-integrated circuit (I²C or simply I2C). A serial connection uses two pins—one to send data (TX) and one to receive data (RX). You should be able to connect any device that supports a serial port (COM port on computers), provided you negotiate the speed (baud rate) and other connection parameters.

SPI uses quite a few pins, but the good news is that it only requires one pin for each SPI device you add to your controller. SPI requires a master and slave role. The microcontroller board will be the master, and the connected devices will be the slaves. With a bit of magic, it's possible to have more than one master device in a system, so if you run into a scenario that requires that, you should do some research on it. Typically, though, you won't need this.

The first SPI pin is the synchronized clock pin (SCK or SCLK). This means that the devices don't need to agree on a preferred speed beforehand. The next two are used for sending and receiving data: Master In Slave Out (MISO) and Master Out Slave In (MOSI). The last one is the Slave Select pin (SS).

By default, all SS lines should be set to high (1, on, or powered). In this state, no device will be communicated with over SPI. To communicate with a specific device, you must set its SS pin to low (0 or off). You can then use the MISO and MOSI pins to communicate with the device.

Wiring multiple devices for SPI is also quite simple. All SCLK pins of the devices will connect to the same SCLK pin on your microcontroller. The same goes for the MISO and MOSI pins. Each SS pin, however, will get its own microcontroller pin.

I²C only requires two pins, called Serial Clock (SCL) and Serial Data (SDA). Simply connect all your I²C devices to these pins on your microcontroller and they will be able to communicate. There is no need to select a device to communicate with since the underlying protocol deals with this. You can connect a maximum of 128 devices in this manner. Each device will be assigned an address (0–127), which should be used to communicate with a specific device.

The actual programming of these microcontrollers is beyond the scope of this book, but there are several well-written books and online resources that cover this subject. Since there are a lot of code samples for all the popular sensors, you won't need to code these from scratch; however, you'll need to be able to understand enough coding to put multiple code samples together and structure your main application to be functional for your setup.

In the next section I'll go over some of the sensors and other components you can connect to these controllers and discuss how to use them. But before you jump into that, take note that sensors require specific voltages. The voltages supplied by the various microcontroller boards also differ. Typical voltages are 3.3V and 5V. Try to match the sensor voltages with the microcontroller you've selected; otherwise, you might need to step the voltage up or down, which would require additional components. Some sensors allow a voltage range, so they might be compatible with most microcontrollers.

ATTINY SERIES CHIP

As you add more sensors and other components to your controller, you can quickly run into a scenario where even a large microcontroller doesn't have enough pins. The ATTiny chip series allows you to extend your board, or it can be used on its own for simple tasks since it has its own programmable memory.

It's basically an even simpler version of the Arduino controller, and it uses same programming language. Uploading code isn't as simple as it is with the Arduino, however, because there isn't a controller board. You will need to get a chip socket to plug it into, and you can then wire it up to your Arduino to flash your program to it. There are some tutorials online that can show you how to do this.

These chips come in many varieties, but all of them have extremely limited resources, so the code should be kept to a minimum. They are particularly useful for dealing with an isolated function, such as only being responsible for regulating water temperature.

Smaller ones come with as few as eight pins (of which six are usable), but one of the most popular ones is the ATTiny2313 chip, which has twenty pins; two of these pins are for power, leaving eighteen usable pins. It has 2KB of ROM for your code and only 128 bytes of RAM, but this is more than enough for simple tasks.

A major advantage of these is that they are very inexpensive. Usually they are sold in batches of twenty or fifty for only a few dollars.

SHIFT REGISTERS

Shift registers might share some visual similarities with the ATTiny chips, but they are very simple chips that can't be programmed. Their purpose is fixed but very useful.

If you have multiple devices that you need to turn on and off, a shift register will allow you to do this with just two pins on your microcontroller board.

If you have an 8-bit shift register, you'll be able to control eight separate devices. Shift registers use one pin to indicate that you want to write a new state to it, and the other pin is used to write the byte value to the register. For example, if you write the byte value 123 to the register, it will be interpreted as the binary value 0111 1011. It will then turn on all the pins corresponding to 1 and turn off all pins corresponding to 0. In this case, six pins will be turned on and two will be turned off.

A good use for these would be to control multiple water pumps to irrigate your crops. Another example would be to control multiple stepper motors, which can be used to control a robotic arm. As noted in the discussion about the SPI communication protocol on page 88, each slave device requires its own pin (SS). This is the perfect scenario in which a shift register could reduce the number of pins used by slave devices.

These chips are simple to use and extremely inexpensive, so you can buy a large batch of them and save a bunch of pins on your microcontrollers. Have a look at a few coding examples of these and play around with them before integrating them into your design. If you're interested in a good model to start with, have a look at the 74HC595N shift register.

REAL-TIME CLOCK MODULE

To save space, microcontrollers typically don't have real-time clocks. When you switch them on, they will reset to an initial date and time, so the current time is lost as soon as you switch them off.

The solution is to add a real-time clock (RTC) module, as it uses a battery to keep the clock powered when the controller board is switched off. These RTC modules often also have a more accurate clock than the onboard ones.

SD-CARD MODULE

The SD-card module is an SPI device that will give you access to the file system on an SD card. If you have a Raspberry Pi controller, you already have one of these as part of the board. This is very useful for logging data from all your sensors or for storing and retrieving configuration information. Since you can't monitor the system 24/7, you'll need to rely on your logs to let you know if something happened since the last time you checked. A new system often incurs some unexpected issues for which you'll need to make adjustments. Logs can point out these problem areas.

The file format of your logs is up to you. A simple approach is to use a comma-delimited format. Start with a time-stamp value and put each sensor in a separate column. You don't need to store the sensor's name, since you'll always put the same sensor in the same column. Each row in the file will be a new reading of all the sensors. Because sensor intervals differ, you can choose to only fill in the columns for the sensors that were measured, or you could keep track of the latest value of all sensors and output whatever the latest value was.

It's a good idea to store logs in text format so that you can easily read them with a text editor if needed. SD cards have very large capacities compared to the amount of data that will be logged, so there's no need to encode or compress it.

You should also split your logs into multiple files instead of logging to a single file. Storing a file a day will work well. Note that after a few years, your folder will have thousands of files and could take some time to load. To avoid this, create a folder for each year.

WI-FI MODULE

For Arduino boards, you will need a Wi-Fi module if you require Internet or LAN connectivity. The Raspberry Pi comes with one built-in.

Make sure you get a module with a connector for an antenna because the ones with built-in antennas can be quite weak and there isn't an option to upgrade to a more powerful antenna. Some Wi-Fi modules have a connector mounted on the board where you can directly connect an antenna. Others will have a small connector for a patch connector to which you can attach an antenna.

The Wi-Fi module communicates via a serial connection with the microcontroller board. You will need to get the datasheet to find out which commands to send to it, or you will need to locate some code samples for your specific model.

LCD DISPLAY

When you check your hydroponic system, it could be very helpful to be able to see your system's current health and status by simply looking at a display. LEDs are also useful for reporting system status, but they are quite limited in what they can convey.

There are several mini LCD displays available for these microcontrollers, but some are a bit difficult to work with and documentation or code samples are not always available. Before you buy one, see if you can find anything on the model you're interested in. Some LCD displays use a serial connection to communicate with the controller board, but there are SPI and I²C ones available as well.

The real estate for the screen is quite limited on these displays, but it should be enough for an overview and warnings. You could add buttons to make it more interactive. For example, with one button, you could have it page through multiple info screens. With more buttons, you can add basic navigation with menus to provide you with more detailed information or to execute basic instructions, such as overriding vent controls to force the vents to open or close.

Adding buttons will consume pins, so you might want to keep this to a minimum. You can also get a multibutton analog module. These typically come with four or five buttons, each connected to a different-sized resistor or chain of resistors, resulting in a specific voltage reading for each button. It will cost you one analog pin, of which there are few, but it would save multiple pins that could be used for other purposes.

RJ45 AND RJ11 JACKS

You will need to run data lines between your microcontroller and sensors or other components. The best way to do this is to use RJ11 (telephone) or RJ45 (LAN) cables. RJ11 can have up to six wires, but they typically have two to four. RJ45 uses eight wires.

You don't need to stick with the standards defined for these connectors, so you can use them as you please. If you don't need all the wires, you can simply leave them disconnected. A four-pin RJ11 cable is a good way to connect an SPI device to your microcontroller, or you can connect five SPI devices with a single RJ45 cable (MISO, MOSI, SCK, and 5x SS).

The cables are designed to carry data signals over some distance and are twisted to reduce cross talk. They aren't ideal for carrying power, so separate lines should be used for that.

You could have a very tidy setup if you house your sensors or components in premanufactured electronic enclosures. You can buy these in various sizes, and they are quite affordable. RJ45 or RJ11 ports, as well as power ports, can then be mounted so that you can easily connect or disconnect devices. It will improve your flexibility if you need to move things around.

BACKUP POWER

A prolonged power failure could be devastating to your hydroponic crop. If you have a system that relies on water pumps, you basically only have until the next irrigation cycle to restore your power, although the crop will likely be fine if it misses one or two cycles. For an aeroponic system, constant irrigation is required, so the pumps need to operate continuously. The water culture system relies just as heavily on its air pump, although this is less critical in other systems.

You'll need to ensure that you have a battery backup system in place that can operate your pumps for at least eight to twelve hours. During a power failure, it might not be possible to power all your equipment, so you would need to have a power-saving profile for your system. For example, you could extend the intervals between irrigation cycles a bit, and instead of running air pumps continuously, you could turn them on and off at intervals to reduce their power consumption by 50 percent. If the batteries start to run low, you can shut them off completely as an emergency measure.

You should also shut off grow lights, since they will consume the most electricity. The plants might not be happy about this, but they will most likely survive. This is not a concern if you use natural light.

If you automated the process of replacing the nutrient tanks as well, you might defer this operation until the power is restored. Temperature control will also have to be suspended. If you have automated vents, they could still be opened and closed since that won't use too much energy, provided you don't open or close them very often. Similarly, any automated blinds or shade cloths can also be operated from a battery.

You will need to take stock of your system and decide which devices are critical, which ones can be scaled back, and which ones can be disabled. When your battery bank drops to 20 percent, you should only operate your critical devices and disable everything else. Note that this critical level will vary depending on the type of battery you use. Lithium-ion batteries can be operated until they're almost completely drained, but lead-acid batteries will be damaged at very low levels. Normal lead-acid batteries for cars should not be drained below 50 percent, so this is your 0 percent level in practical terms. This means that 60 percent will be your 20 percent mark. Deep-cycle batteries are recommended instead, since they can be pushed a bit further than the 50 percent level and will last longer.

Calculate the power consumption of your system in power-saving mode. You can do this by placing your system in that state and measuring the consumption with a watt meter. Alternatively, you can look at the specification of each device and calculate its consumption. This will give you an idea of what size of battery you will need.

Note that if you have AC devices, you'll need an inverter to run from a battery bank. They typically require a 12V or 24V battery bank, so this might affect your configuration. Be aware that the less-expensive ones use a modified sine wave, which outputs a harsh square AC signal. There are some AC devices that can't operate on this kind of AC supply, so do some research before buying one of these. The alternative ones generate a pure sine wave, but they are much more expensive. For DC, you would potentially need to step down your voltage to the correct level, depending on the needs of your devices.

To keep your batteries topped up when the power is on, use a car battery charger. Depending on the model you get, you could leave it connected to the batteries permanently. The charger can detect the battery's status and will trickle a charge to keep the battery bank topped up.

With a battery backup system, the easiest setup is to always run your system from the battery bank and constantly top it up with the battery charger. If the power fails, there is no interruption when switching your system from your mains to your battery bank. Alternatively, you can find automatic failover switches at hardware or solar stores, but these are surprisingly costly. If you do go this route, make sure that you get one that can switch the amount of current required by your system.

Note that there will be some small delay of a few milliseconds when switching circuits. This could cause your equipment to power cycle. For larger power consumers, such as pumps, fans, and heaters, this isn't really a problem, and your operation will continue with nothing more than a stutter, if that.

Your microcontroller won't cope as well. If the system was busy with an operation and the power is cycled, it might not be able to pick up where it left off, and some of your components will be in an unknown state. To prevent this, I suggest adding a separate smaller battery backup for your microcontroller. You can run most of the sensors off of it as well.

A good battery backup for your microcontroller system would consist of rechargeable 18650 lithium cells, as well as a battery holder bay for them. Two to four of these should be enough to run your controller system for a while. To charge them, get a 2A lithium battery charger controller. This can be plugged into your mains to keep the batteries charged. These batteries are more expensive than regular AA batteries but not by a significant margin, so replacing them isn't really an issue.

Your microcontroller would need to be able to detect when your system switches to battery backup so it can activate your power-saving mode. An easy way to do this is to get an AC current sensor. A current sensor is a noninvasive way to measure current and is usually appropriate for higher-current AC environments, such as household appliances. The insulated wire is threaded through the hole of the sensor. To do this you will need to remove the plug of the appliance. For your hydroponic system, the best piece of equipment on which to do this measurement is the battery bank charger.

You will be able to detect the current while your AC supply is online. The reading will drop to zero during a power failure.

The added advantage of measuring the current of your battery charger is that if you are running your system from the battery bank constantly (not using an automatic failover switch), you will be able to calculate the total power consumption of your system because all electricity consumed must go through the battery charger. Since you know what the voltage is (it should be relatively stable), you can multiply this by the amperage to get watts. You can measure this at very regular intervals and log an average over a predetermined period, such as every minute or every ten minutes. This will provide you with very useful information on the electricity consumption of your system and will identify peak periods.

SYSTEM ALARM

Your hydroponic system will run unattended most of the time, so if something more serious goes wrong, you would need to know about it. The pumps are the most important components of the system, so you should find some way to ensure that they are all in working order. This can be detected indirectly by monitoring soil moisture sensors.

If your system detects a dry moisture sensor and activates the pumps but the moisture sensor continues to read as dry, this could be an indication that a pump has failed. You could also use a current sensor to measure the electric current used by the pump. If this sensor reading drops to zero, the pump most likely failed. This sensor can also be used for monitoring air pumps.

If you've automated adding water to your system, you should monitor your water level. For example, if you use a floating valve to keep your tank topped up, you know that the water should always be at a certain level. This can be detected by a water sensor.

If the water sensor isn't returning a reading (meaning it's dry), you might have a problem with your water supply.

A power failure is another crucial system state that should be reported. This becomes even more critical if the batteries run down to 20 percent of the available capacity.

In general, any sensor reading that is significantly outside the defined bounds or that causes you to struggle to correct it should be reported. For instance, if the water temperature is too high and your water-cooling system doesn't seem to have any effect, this could indicate a problem.

When a warning state is detected, someone needs to be informed. The system should raise an audible warning tone by emitting a repetitive beep to get the attention of someone who can attend to it. Microcontroller boards typically don't have built-in buzzers or speakers, so you'll need to get an external one. These are very simple and inexpensive devices. The pins are simply one for positive, one for ground, and another one that's an analog data pin to send the tone to the buzzer. A low voltage will emit a low tone, and a high voltage will emit a high tone. You can play around with it to decide on the kind of beeps you want it to emit. They can be customized for specific types of warnings as well.

LEDs are also popular status indicators. They are very easy to work with and are probably the first thing you will learn about in a microcontroller tutorial.

Beeps and LEDs won't help much if you're not close enough to hear or see them. For that reason, you should have some other means to get notified. Sending an email could be a viable option if you have a Wi-Fi module. You can then include more detailed information and provide a status report on the entire system.

Note that Arduino controllers don't have built-in email functions, so you would have to work with TCP/IP connections directly and build up the raw email messages. You will need to find a sample online if you're not familiar with how to do this.

An easier way might be to just get a GSM module. These devices use a mobile SIM card, allowing you to make voice calls, send messages, or connect to the Internet, even if Wi-Fi is not available, using a mobile data connection. You connect to it via a serial connection. The exact instructions you send will either be provided by the manufacturer or you can find the datasheet on the manufacturer's website.

There should also be a few samples available online. With this, a good option would be to have a text message (SMS) sent to you if something goes wrong. If you want to get fancy, you could write an app for your phone that allows you to receive notifications from your system. You will likely also need a web server to have a known central point to communicate with from your system, as well as from the phone app. The reason for this is that the IP addresses for your phone and hydroponic system are dynamic, so they will change often. A server will have a known address that you can set in your application and in your hydroponic system's configuration.

You can host the server at home if you don't want to pay hosting fees. There are services you can use that will issue a static web address for you so you can access your home-based server via a fixed URL from any computer.

Of course, with a mobile app, the door is opened to do much more than just receive warning messages. You can also actively monitor the system and instruct it to do certain tasks if you wish. If you have experience in developing mobile apps, this could be a valuable addition to your system.

RELAYS

A relay is basically just a switch that you can turn on or off electronically. The circuits inside are isolated from each other, so you can use a low-powered signal from your controller to turn on a separately powered circuit.

There are many different types of relays, so check the specifications carefully before ordering. Some relays will be labeled "normally open" (NO) or "normally closed" (NC). This indicates its state when no signal is sent (its off state). NO is the easiest to understand; if you send an on/1 signal, the controlled circuit will turn on as well. NC will be on by default and will turn off your controlled circuit if you send a signal to it.

Relays are rated as SPST, SPDT, DPST, or DPDT. The simplest option is SPST, which stands for "single pole, single throw." It's the equivalent of a basic switch you can find on a bed lamp. It works by simply disconnecting one of the wires. In the bed lamp example, this would either be the live or neutral wire.

On the other end of the spectrum there is DPDT or "double pole, double throw." The double-pole portion means that it will switch two wires simultaneously. This could be either on the same circuit or from separate circuits. In the bed lamp example, it would be the equivalent of having a switch on the live and neutral wires and flipping them simultaneously.

The double-throw portion means that instead of breaking the circuit or engaging it, it will switch between separate circuits. This is more like a toggle switch. If you had two separate bed lamps, you could connect a double-throw relay to toggle between one lamp or the other. Only one of them will be powered at a time.

Figure 6.1 (left) shows the difference between the various relay options.

Buying a relay module that's compatible with Arduino or Raspberry Pi will allow you to connect it directly to your controller board to switch it, but you will need to power your board with an external power source that can supply enough amperage to trigger the unit. Some modules require a 12V DC supply to trigger it and a relatively high current compared to what these controller boards can supply. You might need to connect

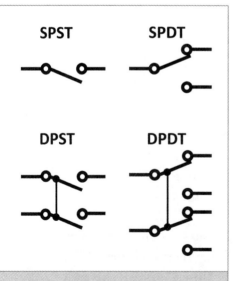

FIG. 6.1 Different types of relays

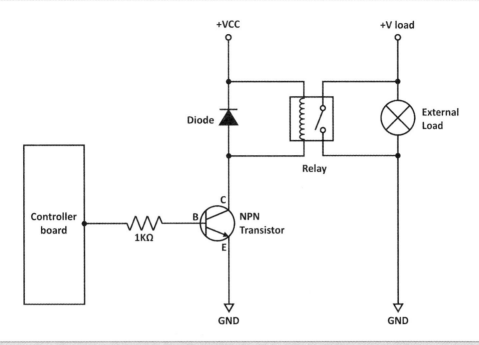

FIG. 6.2 Example of a controller board and relay model

the relay to its own power supply and use a transistor to switch the relay.

The exact components you'll need will depend on the controller you're using and the relay specifications. A basic setup will look something like figure 6.2 (above).

If you're not familiar with transistors, you'll need to read up on them before building a circuit like this. A diode should be added to relays and motors if there could potentially be reverse feedback. The diode should also be correctly sized for the circuit.

SOLENOID VALVE

A solenoid valve is a liquid or gas valve that you can open or close with an electronic signal. It's the relay equivalent of liquid or gas pipes. In a hydroponic system, it can be used to control the flow of CO_2 gas from a cylinder or to top up a tank with water from your mains if you're not using some other mechanism, such as a float valve.

On page 75, I discussed a water-saving technique in which you allow the nutrient tank level to drop to an almost depleted level before flushing it and replacing it. This operation would require using a solenoid because a float valve won't work in this situation. Instead, you would control the freshwater supply from the mains with a solenoid valve. You can also control the draining of the tank with a solenoid and allow gravity to empty the tank.

A solenoid valve is also useful if you have a single nutrient tank for multiple crops with different irrigation intervals. You can then use a single pump and a solenoid for each irrigation line. Make sure that you buy a good-quality solenoid to avoid leakage. The ones that mostly consist of plastic might have shorter life-spans and have leakage issues.

As with relays, solenoids are normally open (NO) and normally closed (NC). Some will also resemble the "double-throw" property of some relays in which the solenoid valve toggles between one of two pathways instead of opening and closing.

Solenoid valves can be a bit expensive, especially if you buy a good-quality one. Some could cost as much as a low-end water pump, so take this into consideration when you're deciding how to build your system.

TEMPERATURE SENSOR

The temperature sensor module is one of the simplest sensors. It's available in a few varieties, with the primary differences being accuracy and scale. Most are suitable for typical ambient ranges, but even if one goes out of range, it means that your growing area is very far beyond what is acceptable for the plants. There are variants of these modules that can measure humidity as well.

Typically, when you see a three-pin sensor, one pin is the supply voltage (3.3V or 5V), one is the ground, and the other is the signal pin. The signal pin will return an analog voltage ranging from 0V to the maximum input voltage. The specification sheet of the module will let you know what the scale is.

Specification sheets are very helpful in this regard, so seek them out whenever possible. Alternatively, search for the specific model number online. The supplier will most likely also be able to help you. This information is sometimes available on the order page.

As an example, suppose the temperature range of the sensor is 32–212 degrees F (0–100 degrees C). If you purchased a 5V module, your signal pin will output a voltage of 1.25V at 77 degrees F (25 degrees C).

A water-temperature probe basically works in the same manner. It has three wires instead of the pins. The one end has a hollow waterproof metal tube with the same temperature sensor as the ones used on the Arduino modules. In your growing room, you should ideally have one water-temperature probe per nutrient tank, but one might suffice for a small area if all tanks are protected from direct sunlight.

You should have at least one ambient-temperature sensor module to ensure your growing area is operating at ideal temperatures. You would need more than one in a large space and should ideally have one in direct light, one in the shade, and one in the root area of the crop. Placing one outside the growing area will let you know what effect venting will have on the temperature inside your growing area.

You should use your microcontroller to log the data to an SD card or to upload it to the cloud via Wi-Fi, GSM/mobile, or an Ethernet cable. The interval is up to you. The data will let you know how often your plants are in distressed ranges and can help you to decide how to deal with that.

Logging is one thing, but being able to react based on the temperature is much more useful. This is quite easy with a microcontroller. You use an AC relay to turn on circulating or extracting fans if the temperature goes above a specific threshold, and you can turn on a heater if the temperature drops below a specified minimum threshold. It can also be used to control automatic shutters and vents if you have those in your growing area.

It's not so useful for turning on air-conditioning units since these already have temperature controllers and aim to keep the temperature constant, which is exactly what you want in a growing area. Furthermore, air conditioners tend to start up in a specific mode, and you would need a remote control to set it to a different mode. If you decide to go this route, you could do this with an IR module by simulating the key presses of the remote control. You would first need to record the pulses with an IR receiver module. Once you have those, you'll need to play them back via the IR LED. It might be a bit tricky to get the timing right. These modules are very inexpensive and the process is quite simple, so if you really wish to control an air-conditioning unit, you would be able to do so with your microcontroller.

You can also add a mister to your growing area to cool it down, but this would raise the humidity, so be careful with this option. The misting system should be connected to a water tank with a water pump. The microcontroller can then turn on the pump via a relay if necessary. You can keep the water tank topped up with a floating valve, like the ones used in toilets.

If your code is a bit smarter, you could have multiple strategies for cooling or heating based on the current temperature levels and running costs involved. If humidity is low, it could be more cost-efficient to use the mister. You can then start powering up circulation fans if the temperature is not dropping enough. If you have a temperature sensor on the outside as well as on the inside of your growing area, you could evaluate whether to open or close vents and when to use extractor fans.

As you can see, there's quite a bit of coding that can go into just controlling the temperature.

HUMIDITY SENSOR

The humidity sensor module is another useful addition to your hydroponic system. The most popular model is the DHT11, but the DHT22 is more accurate. The DHT11 and DHT22 sensors have built-in temperature sensors as well, so this could replace your temperature-only sensor.

Both will accept a 3–5V input voltage, so it's ideal for most controllers. The DHT11's humidity range is a bit limited since it can only report on a range of 20–80 percent humidity with a 5 percent accuracy rating. The DHT22 covers the full range (0–100 percent) with a 2–5 percent accuracy rate. The DHT11 has a temperature range of 32–122 degrees F (0–50 degrees C) and an accuracy rating of 35 degrees F (2 degrees C). This is acceptable in a hydroponic environment. The DHT22 ranges between -40 degrees F (-40 degrees C) and 257 degrees F (125 degrees C) and has an accuracy rating of 32 degrees F (0.5 degrees C).

Reading the information from the data pin is slightly trickier because you'll need to read two values from it. Luckily, this is a well-known sensor and there is a library you can use that will return the humidity and temperature readings.

PELTIER THERMOELECTRIC UNIT

In chapter 4, page 55, I mentioned how to control the water temperature using a Peltier thermoelectric unit. You simply connect the correct power supply to it, and it will heat up on one side while cooling the other side. Two mini aluminium water tanks are fastened to each side. These are called water cooling blocks and can be purchased at computer hardware stores. You would also need a water pump for each of these water blocks.

Water blocks can often fit multiple Peltier units, and I recommend doing that to speed up water heating or cooling. Each Peltier unit has an inlet and an outlet connector on the top. Remember to add thermal paste between the Peltier unit and the water blocks, as this will help with heat exchange.

To automate your water-temperature management, connect the water pumps and Peltier unit with separate relays. Be sure to use the correct relays for this. Check whether you need AC or DC relays and verify that they can handle the voltage and amperage. Finally, you'll also need a water-temperature probe.

When the water is within the ideal range, everything will be turned off. As soon as it crosses a threshold, turn on the Peltier unit and start to circulate water through the correct tank by turning on the relevant water pump. The water pumps can be set to a slow speed, since it will take time for heat to be exchanged, so circulating the water rapidly isn't very useful. Note that heat exchange happens faster at larger temperature differentials, so don't slow down the pump to a crawl either.

The pumps will run until the water is all the way back to the ideal temperature. At that point, the pumps and the Peltier unit will be turned off and allowed to drift until either threshold is triggered again.

WATER FLOW METER

The water flow meter is a very basic component that measures the amount of water that passes through it. In a hydroponic system, this can be useful for a number of reasons.

First, it's good to keep track of how much water your system is using. This can help you determine which system is more effective and has the least waste. A water meter can also keep track of the amount of water you're discarding. The difference will reflect the amount consumed by your crop. Furthermore, if you use moisture sensors to trigger irrigation, the water flow meter would provide a way for you to keep track of the amount of water the plants received during the day or each hour.

Second, the water flow meter can be used to detect problems with a pump or valve. If there is no water flowing when you expect it to flow, or if there's too little or too much water, it could indicate a problem.

As usual, red is the positive wire and black is the ground wire. The other wire (yellow, white, or something else) would be the data pin (or the water flow meter). It works by sending a single electrical pulse for each revolution completed by the internal rotor.

Each flow meter will do a certain number of revolutions per quart/liter of water that passes through it. Its datasheet should indicate this. You can then calculate the current flow rate by dividing the number of revolutions by the time that has passed since you started the measurement. This means that prior to taking a measurement, you need to decide how many seconds you are going to perform this measurement before a result is returned. The longer the period, the more accurate the reading will be, but a reading over a few seconds should be fine.

The pulses from these sensors are very short, and they could easily be missed if you try to actively read the values from the pin. Also, your code won't be able to do anything else during that period. To override this, you'll need to use a special pin called an interrupt pin. You will need to check your microcontroller's documentation to see if it has such pins and where they are located. These pins will allow you to run your code and perform other tasks, but as soon as you receive a signal on the interrupt pin, it will interrupt your main code and execute a specified function. These must be very short and simple functions; otherwise, they will block other interrupts.

With an interrupt, you can simply program a counter to count the number of revolutions. Keep track of the time stamp when you started the counter. You can then calculate how many gallons/liters passed through the water meter since you started the counter. This will give you an overall measurement, but it won't be able to provide you with information on the current flow rate of your meter. For this, you will need a second counter and timer that resets every five to ten seconds. This will give you a count over the last few seconds, which you can use to calculate the current water flow rate.

SOIL MOISTURE SENSOR

The soil moisture sensor is very simple to use. With a module, it will return a digital signal (high or low, depending on its design) if a certain level of conductivity (that is, at a specific moisture level) has been detected. On the model, you will typically find a potentiometer that you can adjust to set the sensitivity of the sensor. The pins are simply the supply voltage, ground, and a digital data pin.

If you remove the module with the potentiometer and connect the moisture sensor directly to the microcontroller, you can connect its data pin to an analog pin to get an analog reading. This could be useful to detect various moisture levels of your growing medium. You can calibrate your controller by first measuring the completely dry growing medium (the measurement should be close to zero) and gradually adding moisture until it's completely saturated. As you add moisture, take note at what level you would want to trigger the irrigation to start. This would be the lowest acceptable moisture level for your crops. Next, take note at which level you would stop irrigation when the crop has enough moisture. Your code should trigger irrigation to start when it drops below the lower threshold and stop irrigation when it rises above the upper threshold.

Unfortunately, there are a limited number of analog pins, so it might be too expensive to use them for moisture sensors. An alternative is to use two digital pins and two moisture sensors with their modules. You can set one moisture sensor to the lower threshold level and the other one to the upper threshold. This will cost you two digital pins, but there should be more of these available. It would also cost you an additional sensor, but they are quite inexpensive and are often bought in bulk.

Your final option is to use a single moisture sensor connected to a digital input pin, which is set to the lower threshold value. You will trigger irrigation to start if this threshold is breached. From there you can determine how long you should run your water pump to sufficiently water the plants. The irrigation period will be timer based. In general, this should be fine, since your pumps should supply a predictable amount of water over a given period. You can monitor it manually to determine how long will be enough and then configure your code accordingly.

Using an analog sensor has the advantage of warning you if something goes wrong in your system. If the reading shows an abnormally dry or abnormally wet growing medium, it could indicate that something went awry. With a single digital sensor, you can only infer this for the dry scenario, because if the sensor still reports a dry medium even after irrigation started, it indicates that a problem occurred, such as a pump failure or blockage.

WATER LEVEL SENSOR

The water level sensor has three pins. Two of them are required for power, and the other one is an analog pin. The analog signal returned is directly proportional to the amount of water that is in contact with its metal strips.

The sensor modules are only a few centimeters in length, so they can only report on a short water level range. A single sensor won't be able to tell you the current level of your nutrient tank.

These sensors are quite useful for shallow tanks or to finely measure the upper water level of the tank. For example, you could use the sensor to control a solenoid to top up the tank if the sensor reads 10 percent of its value range and close the valve at 90 percent. The water level will then fluctuate in that range on the length of the sensor.

If you want to measure the entire length of your tank, you could use multiple sensors to accomplish this. Suppose your tank requires the length of five sensors (the metal strip portion, not the full sensor length), you could add resistors to each sensor, so that the reading will be reduced to 20 percent of the original reading. You can then mount them inside your container in a stepping formation (see figure 6.3).

By connecting them all to a single analog pin, you should be able to get a full range reading if all sensors are submerged. You

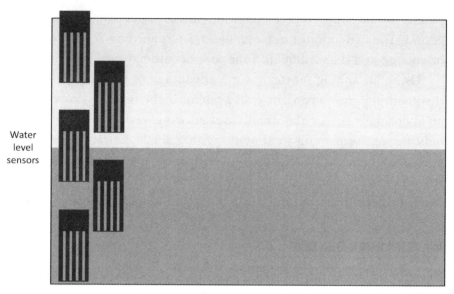

Water
level
sensors

nutrient solution reservoir

FIG. 6.3 Water level sensors

should properly insulate the components on the board, as well as the connectors and wires. Use silicone and a shrink sleeve to create a watertight seal.

Water level sensors are very inexpensive, and you can order them in bulk to reduce costs even further. These sensors are also used as rain sensors. You could use one for the same purpose to detect when it's raining outside your growing area. This could be relevant if you capture rainwater for use in your hydroponic system. This is a viable water source, but remember to filter and sterilize the rainwater before introducing it into your system. Rainwater is typically very pure, but the outside surfaces from which you collect it could introduce debris and pathogens.

LIGHT SENSORS

Measuring the light level in your growing area is important to ensure that your crops get enough light. Cloudy days could leave your crops deprived, so supplementing their need on these days using grow lights is recommended. If you only use artificial light in your growing area, you could also use a light sensor to detect if your lights are working.

For HPS lights, you might want to use a light sensor to monitor the light intensity emitted by your lamps to determine when they need to be replaced. LED lights don't suffer the same fate, but sometimes they fail partially and emit light at a significantly diminished rate (about 10 percent of their total brightness).

When using the sun as a light source, you might also want to monitor your UV levels. High levels could be damaging to your plants. A UV sensor will inform you if you have provided enough UV filtering for your growing area.

The most basic light sensor is the light dependent resistor (LDR), or photoresistor. It works like a normal resistor, except the resistance decreases as light increases. The LDR is an analog sensor, so the pins are quite simple. Two are used for power and the other one for the analog signal.

Although these sensors can provide you with a basic light intensity range, they are not very accurate. They are better at simply detecting whether a certain threshold of light is present. For this reason, some of these sensors will have a potentiometer so that you can set that threshold; these will be digital sensors rather than analog sensors. These are very inexpensive and are therefore ideal to use for failure detection of your grow lights.

If you want to accurately measure the amount of lux in your growing area, you need to use a more-sensitive light sensor, such as the BH1750. The BH1750 uses the I²C interface and returns the light intensity already formatted as lux, so no conversions are required. This is the sensor that you will be using to record the light intensity during the day so you can decide whether you need to supplement the supply with grow lights.

There are a few strategies available when it comes to supplementing natural light with artificial light. This will also depend on the type of grow lights you have. The ideal option is to have multiple low-wattage, full-spectrum LED bulbs that you can control either individually or in small groups. For instance, if you have one hundred bulbs in your growing area, you could connect them in batches of ten bulbs, which would give you ten separate groups to control. You can then use the light intensity sensor to measure the current light level and turn on one group of LEDs at a time until your levels are where they should be. The result will be that your growing area has the perfect amount of light every day, regardless of weather conditions. This is also the most cost-effective option.

An alternative strategy may work better if you have large light units, such as MH lights, HPS lights, or large LED units. For this approach, measure the amount of light and compare it with the expected amount of light at that point of the day. If it is lower than expected but within a decent range, you don't need to turn on the lights yet. Just keep track of this deficiency. You can then predict how much light your crop will receive during the day if light levels remain stable.

Suppose you calculate a prediction of 75 percent if the sun rises at seven o'clock a.m. and sets at seven o'clock p.m. In this situation, you can turn on your grow lights for the last 25 percent of that period, which would be four o'clock p.m. to seven o'clock p.m. (three hours). This also depends on the strength of your lights, since you could have decided to purchase fewer lights if you are mainly going to rely on natural light. Bear in mind the light saturation level of plants, which might increase the number of hours you need to run the lights. As an extreme example, suppose your growing lights could only supply 25 percent of the required light. You would then have had to turn on the growing lights in the morning already since they would only be able to supplement the 25 percent that the natural light level is lacking.

The final light sensor I'll be discussing is the GUVA-S12SD UV sensor.

The pins are very simple since it's a standard analog sensor, meaning that two pins are used for power and the other one is used for an analog data pin. This sensor is less useful than the light intensity sensor because it's typically only needed when you set up your growing area, to ensure that you have enough UV filtering. It could also serve as a warning sensor to detect large ruptures in the greenhouse plastic sheeting and can inform you when the plastic has deteriorated to such an extent that it no longer provides adequate protection.

If you don't have UV filtering in your growing area and make use of blinds or shade covers instead, this sensor can be used to detect when UV levels are getting too high and can roll down the blinds or shade covers. The blinds/shade covers can be retracted when levels return to normal. In this scenario, you would combine this sensor with a temperature sensor, so that whenever any of the two sensor readings are beyond a certain threshold, it will roll down the blinds/shade covers. UV is also a valuable statistic to log so that you can determine the optimal levels for each crop.

BAROMETRIC SENSOR

The barometric sensor measures atmospheric pressure, which can be used to calculate elevation (not useful in a hydroponic system) or to make short-term weather predictions. The pins on these sensors could be a bit confusing, but this is because they support both SPI and I^2C, so you can use whichever you prefer. A popular model is the BMP250. It has an accuracy of 1 hPa and includes a temperature sensor that is accurate to 33 degrees F (1 degree C). This is one of those nice-to-have sensors, but your system will be fine without one.

CO_2 SENSOR

CO_2 sensors are quite useful in a hydroponic system and essential if you're using CO_2 cylinders to add CO_2 to your growing area. Unfortunately, they are currently very expensive.

The sensor can be used in analog mode (via its analog pin) to read the current level of CO_2, or you can use its digital pin to trigger only when the CO_2 level rises above a certain setting. On the back of the sensor is a potentiometer screw that you can adjust to the desired threshold for the digital pin.

Since the growing area is an enclosed space, oxygen levels tend to rise during the day, while CO_2 levels drop. The opposite happens at night. So during the day, you'll want to ensure that your plants receive enough CO_2, and during the night, they should receive enough oxygen.

By monitoring the CO_2 levels, you can trigger your extractor fans when the oxygen level starts to rise during the day or when it drops during the night. This would work even better if you have a CO_2 sensor on the inside and outside, because then you would know whether it would be beneficial to turn on the extractor fan.

If you're using a CO_2 cylinder, this will help you maintain the desired level of CO_2 by using a solenoid valve to open and close the cylinder. In the evening, when photosynthesis ceases, you can vent it.

CO_2 levels have a major influence on plant growth. So even though this sensor is expensive, it will pay for itself by allowing you to actively manage the CO_2 levels.

pH PROBE

A pH probe is indispensable for a hydroponic system. Handheld pH probes are economical, but that's not true of the ones that are compatible with microcontroller boards. It's possible to modify handheld pH probes and access the pH reading, but doing so is a bit tricky, and detailed information about this is difficult to get hold of.

The pH probe modules that are compatible with microcontrollers come with a detachable electrode and are secured via a BNC connector.

The module itself is the more expensive of the two parts, which is good news considering that electrodes need to be replaced annually. You don't necessarily need to buy the same model electrode when you replace it, so you can shop around for lower-priced alternatives.

The module uses a serial connection to return the data to the microcontroller. You can also connect it as an I²C device. There are a few different modules, so you might find other interfaces as well. Luckily, the manufacturers of these modules often provide detailed information on their websites, explaining how to take care of the electrode and how to communicate with it.

The sensor accuracy is 0.1 pH and has a range of 1–14 pH, so this is perfect for a hydroponic setup. As I mentioned earlier, these electrodes need to be replaced annually, but they also need to be cleaned and calibrated monthly.

A major problem to overcome when it comes to automation is the fact that you can't leave the pH electrode in the nutrient solution for an extended period. It's only supposed to be used to take a measurement and then be removed. It gets even more complicated since you need to clean the electrode with purified or distilled water before and after you've taken your measurement. You then need to store it in the storage liquid provided until the next use. The storage liquid is the same liquid that can be found inside the electrode, which is usually a potassium chloride (KCl) solution. This is also what you will use if you start to notice that the electrode is drying out. Some electrodes have a refill cap to top them up.

To calibrate the pH electrode, you'll have to use reference liquids at known pH levels. At least two reference liquids, which are typically 4 pH and 7 pH, will be needed. Some manufacturers will also provide you with a third one at 10 pH. Since your hydroponic system will operate in the acidic range, it's not necessary to calibrate the probe with the 10 pH solution as well.

Even though automating the pH measurement in a hydroponic system is a bit complicated, it's not impossible. Doing so will bring you one more step closer to a fully automated system.

See chapter 7, page 120, for more detailed information on automating pH measurements.

EC/TDS PROBE

As with the pH probe, handheld TDS probes are low cost and easily obtainable. TDS probes that are readily usable with a microcontroller board are difficult to find. Although it's possible to modify a handheld TDS probe to get access to the reading, building your own is also an option. There are a few resources online to help you with this process.

TDS electrodes also need to be calibrated. If you purchase a kit online, the calibration liquid will be included. If it isn't, you will need to make your own calibration liquid. This is very easy to do. All you need is a salt, such as potassium chloride (KCl) or sodium chloride (NaCl), and distilled water. Distilled water is essential because it has a ppm reading of zero.

To create a 1,000 ppm calibration solution, dissolve .04 ounces (1 g) of the salt in 1 quart (1 L) of water. Make sure the measurement is exact and that all the salt has completely dissolved; otherwise your calibration liquid will not be accurate. You can create multiple calibration solutions to ensure the probe operates correctly at all concentrations.

If you're building your own TDS probe, consider using a handheld TDS probe's housing and its electrodes. This will ensure that you'll have a decent electrode. These electrodes are typically plated with platinum, gold, or nickel at fixed distances between the electrode pins, allowing for a stable, accurate reading. Some materials can give very inaccurate results and are also more prone to corrosion.

TDS electrodes should not be left submerged in the nutrient solution because corrosion and buildup will be a problem, even if you use a good-quality electrode.

TDS probes don't need to be calibrated as often as pH sensors. Calibrating it once or twice a year should suffice.

Unlike pH meters, you don't need to have clean the probe before and after use, but it's nevertheless good practice, especially if you use the sensor on multiple nutrient tanks. TDS sensors are not kept in the storage liquid but are stored dry instead.

Automating the TDS probe will have obstacles similar to those encountered with the pH probe. In chapter 7, I will address these for both types of probes.

7

the lab

There is no gardening without humility. Nature is constantly sending even its oldest scholars to the bottom of the class for some egregious blunder.

ALFRED AUSTIN

ow that you've learned about all the popular sensors and components that you'll be using in your hydroponic system, it's time to address some of the complications you might encounter with automation. Basically you'll be building a mini automated lab that will be able to measure pH and TDS, calibrate and clean the probes, rebalance pH, and add the correct nutrients in the correct amounts. It should also be able to add hydrogen peroxide when required and chlorine when a tank needs to be sterilized. To accomplish this, you'll need to rely heavily on a special pump known as a dosing pump (also called a peristaltic pump). Dosing pumps are used in laboratories and in the medical industry to pump precise amounts of a liquid. They are rated at a certain amount of milliliters per minute. By running the pump for a specific amount of time, you can calculate the precise amount of milliliters that were displaced.

Medical-grade plastic tubing is used for transporting the liquids. To prevent buildup and chemical interaction, glass containers are used instead of plastic. This isn't essential since some plastic containers are well suited for the specific liquids they're intended to contain, but glass works well for pretty much any liquid and is easier to clean.

Since the probes are expensive, and the dosing pumps aren't cheap either, you'll want to use a single lab unit for all nutrient tanks. Dosing pumps can operate in both directions, so with some planning, it's possible to use a single dosing pump for each nutrient tank.

The lab unit uses three glass beakers to perform its tasks. One is used for measuring the EC, one is used for measuring pH, and the last one is used for nutrient tank additives (nutrient mixtures, pH adjustment, hydroperoxide, and chlorine). The reason why the pH and EC probes can't share a beaker is because the pH probe must be stored in a liquid, while the EC probe must be stored dry.

Figure 7.1 (below) provides a simplistic view of a single dosing pump in a nutrient tank and doesn't show the probes or other pumps you'll be using. Each beaker's processes will be explained separately later in this chapter.

If you turn on the dosing pump to extract some nutrient solution from the nutrient tank, it will start to add equal amounts to each beaker. Figure 7.1 doesn't indicate this, but to be able to add equal amounts, the tubing needs to be the same length to each beaker. Note that the one-way valve and longer tube to the additives beaker will affect the time it takes for the fluid to reach the beaker.

The purpose of the one-way valve is so you can pump the nutrient mixture to the pH and TDS beakers, but when the pump is reversed, it doesn't suck in air. These are not solenoid valves.

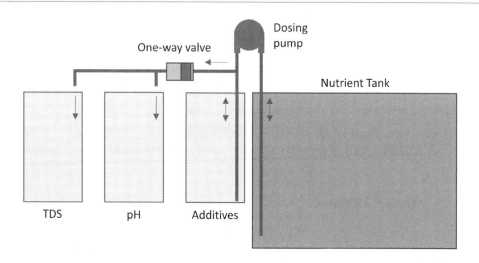

FIG. 7.1 How to use a single dosing pump per nutrient tank

They are passive, inexpensive, and easily obtainable from stores that sell aquarium equipment.

The reason there isn't a longer tube in the additives beaker is because the dosing pump needs to be able to pump fluids to the nutrient tank. The tube needs to touch the bottom of the beaker so you can pump as much of the fluid from the beaker as possible. Just be careful not to create a situation in which the suction causes the tube to stick to the bottom of the beaker, as this would prevent any fluid from being pumped out. You can cut the tip of the tube at an angle or cut a V notch in it to prevent this from occurring.

You don't need to be concerned about this for the pH and TDS beakers since you'll only be adding some nutrient mixture to them. They won't be returned and will be flushed out after the measurements have been made. This is to prevent contamination of the nutrient tank since other fluids will enter those beakers that should not end up in the nutrient mixture. You'll only need small amounts to test the pH and ppm, so it won't affect the nutrient tank levels by much.

There are some limitations when using a single-dosing pump per nutrient tank. The first one is that you'll always pump fluid to all three beakers. This means that you'll need to measure pH and TDS at the same time. This isn't a concern, and it's actually the preferred process. However, you'll have no choice but to pump liquid into the additives beaker, even though it serves no purpose. Adding a one-way valve isn't an option because these valves aren't perfect seals, so some liquid might still enter the beaker. Furthermore, the tube section in front of the one-way valve will still fill up with fluid, so you must reverse the dosing pump in any case. It's better to keep components to a minimum if they can't add enough value.

Use Cases

Now let's run through the use cases of this configuration. Note that the focus will only be on figure 7.1 (page 121). I won't go into any detail about the measurement processes or additive process.

The pH and TDS of a nutrient tank need to be measured simultaneously. To do this, you'll first pump in some nutrient mixture from the nutrient tank, which will start to fill all three beakers. You only need to add the minimum amount required to take both measurements. When the measurement is complete, the dosing pump will need to be reversed to pump the nutrient mixture in the additives beaker back into the nutrient tank. All beakers should then be flushed and cleaned (see page 125–126), and then the lab unit will be ready for its next task.

To adjust the nutrient tank, the fluids involved (which will depend on the type of adjustment required) are put into the additives beaker. Once it is ready, the dosing pump is used to pump it to the nutrient mix. The additives beaker should then be cleaned, after which the lab unit will be ready for its next task.

The Detailed Processes of Each Beaker

The TDS beaker is the easiest, so I'll start with that one. The dosing pump in figure 7.2 (page 124) that's taking in nutrient solution from the nutrient tank is the same dosing pump from figure 7.1 (page 121), just without all the other components. The purified waterline is also one that you'll see in other figures. It's used to clean the beakers. Since you'll clean all the beakers at the same time, this is also a shared dosing pump. Therefore, when you see it in other figures, it represents the same dosing pump.

The TDS beaker will be cleaned after a TDS reading has taken place or after a calibration has been performed. When you run a cleaning process, you don't have to fill the entire beaker, but you do need to add ample water to properly dilute any waste fluid that was present in the beaker.

You'll notice that there is an air pump as well. This is part of the cleaning process, and since cleaning occurs at the same time for all beakers, you can share this pump with all of them. Once you have filled the beaker to the desired level with purified water,

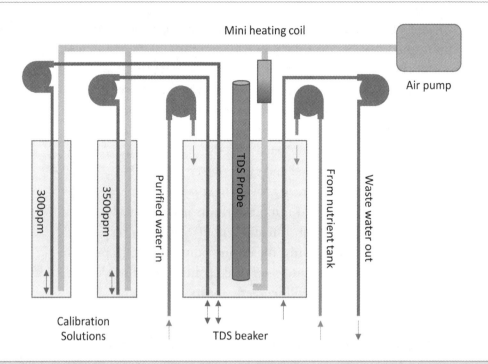

FIG. 7.2 All the parts involved for the TDS beaker

you can start the air pump to agitate the water. This helps with rinsing the probe.

In figure 7.2 (above), a heating coil is installed on the airflow line running to the beaker. This is used to help dry the beaker and probe. The coil isn't a critical component if you're not taking measurements very often, but you don't want any moisture to remain in the beaker by the next time you take a measurement, especially when you are doing a calibration, as this could contaminate the calibration liquid.

You might struggle to find a suitable heating coil for this setup, but it's not difficult to make your own. All you need is some heating coil wire, which you can purchase from a hardware store or online. The ones used in e-cigarettes work well for this. You can place these coils on the inside of a metal tube. The metal tube doesn't need to be a good heat conductor since you'll rely only on the coils for heat. You will need to find a way to properly connect the metal tube to your silicone tubing to ensure that you have an airtight seal. Test the temperature of the air with the coils turned on. It should not be scalding hot— just warm enough to sufficiently evaporate the remaining drops of water.

The air pump also flows to the calibration reservoirs. By bubbling air in the calibration reservoirs at the same time the beakers are being cleaned, you'll help to prevent sediment from forming. If you don't do measurements regularly, you might want to allow the air pump to run for a several minutes a few extra times a day. Once you're done with the rinsing, drain out the beaker using the wastewater dosing pump.

In figure 7.2 there are two calibration solutions. Values of 300 ppm and 3,500 ppm have been chosen because that's the range of concentration for the various crops listed on page 76, but you can change this range to the ranges required by your specific crops instead. Two calibration liquids should be enough.

Note that the tubes for the calibration liquid go all the way down to the bottom of the beaker. This is because you'll be returning the calibration liquid to its reservoir once it's been calibrated.

Two Use Cases for the TDS Beaker

The first use case is for taking a TDS measurement. To do this, add a small amount of nutrient solution from the nutrient tank, and use the probe to do the measurement. Discard the nutrient solution sample and add water to the beaker to rinse it out. Use the air pump without the heating coil to help with the rinsing. Discard the water and use the air pump with the heating coil to assist with the evaporation of any remaining drops.

The second use case is the calibration of the TDS probe. Pump the first calibration solution into the beaker and take the measurement. Use the reading as the first new reference value and store it. Pump the calibration liquid back into its reservoir and rinse the beaker using the purified waterline and air pump without the heating coil. Flush out the water via the waste line and run the air pump with the heating coils to dry the beaker and probe. Repeat this process for the second calibration liquid. If you don't have heating coils, you'll need to wait a while for the last few drops to evaporate naturally before you can calibrate with the second calibration liquid.

Your calibration liquid reservoirs need to be large enough so they won't dilute too much if they do come in contact with a few drops of liquid. A drop is generally considered to be .007 ounces (.05 ml), which isn't much, and since you won't be calibrating your TDS probe often, this might be an acceptable level of contamination.

The pH Beaker

F igure 7.3 (below) illustrates the processes of the pH beaker. You'll notice that it's familiar because it has the same use-cases as the TDS beaker: taking a nutrient solution measurement

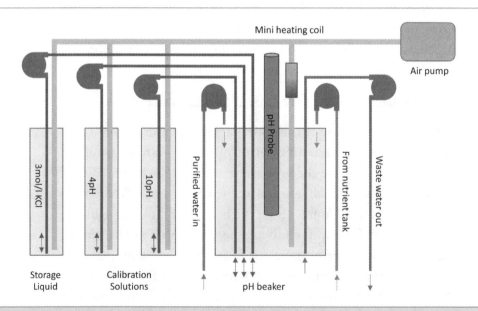

FIG. 7.3 The process of the pH beaker

and performing a calibration. Therefore, I'll only discuss the differences between the TDS beaker and the pH beaker.

The first difference, which might not be obvious, is that the pH probe is a bit raised compared to the TDS probe. Also, the air nozzle is pointing downward and not toward the probe. That's because you don't want to dry out the pH probe; you only want to evaporate any liquid residue in the beaker. In this case, the heating coil is highly recommended, because you'll want to dry out the beaker as quickly as possible and then fill it with the storage solution.

Whenever the probe is not in use, it must be stored in the storage solution, which is 3 mol/L of KCl solution in this situation. You will need to verify what electrolyte your pH probe uses so that you can use the same storage solution. The manufacturer might have included some storage solution, but it's a good idea to find out exactly what they provided in case you need to replace it.

The calibration solutions I recommend are a 4 pH solution, which is an acid, and a 10 pH solution, which is an alkaline. The calibration solutions provided by the manufacturer of the probe might differ. For example, a popular one is 7 pH, which is distilled water. This means that you could potentially use your purified waterline as a calibration solution, but only if you are using distilled water. If your water quality varies (even though it's purified), it will not suffice as a replacement calibration liquid.

The air pump, nutrient pump, and purified water pump are the same pumps shown in figure 7.2 (page 124), but the wastewater lines in the figures can't be shared. You won't be able to properly drain all the beakers if one of them empties first and starts to introduce air into the system. Air won't be a problem if only one body of liquid is involved.

Note that it's possible to use the same heating coil unit. You simply need to install a splitter after the coil. Something to consider, though, is that every time you do a pH probe calibration (which should be monthly), you will also need to fill the TDS beaker with water every time you fill the pH beaker. This is fine, provided you remember to also run the TDS beaker's waste pump to pump it out. The air pump will then dry both beakers. This is an annoying consequence of shared pumps. It's harmless, but it's something you need to be aware of to ensure that you handle it appropriately.

The Additives Beaker

Figure 7.4 (below) illustrates the various processes of the additives beaker. Once again, you will notice that there are many similarities with figures 7.2 (page 124) and 7.3 (page 126), except there are significantly more reservoirs. The water and waste lines work the same way as with the other beakers. In this case, you'll need to flush them out with purified water after you've made the necessary adjustments to the nutrient reservoir. The air pump and heat coil are used in the same way as with the pH and TDS units.

With the additives beaker, the nutrient solution line goes all the way to the bottom because you'll need to be able to add the mixture to the nutrient tank. As shown in figure 7.4 (below), the nutrient solution is drawn from the nutrient tank. Since the addi-

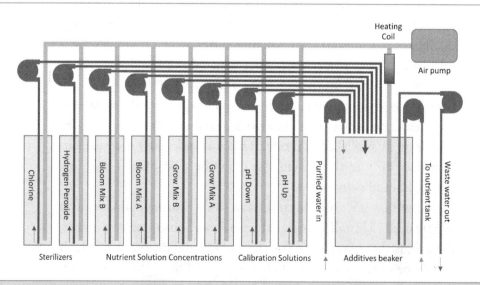

FIG. 7.4 The various processes of the additives beaker

tives beaker is only used for adding to the nutrient tank and not used to take measurements of the current nutrient mixture in the tank, drawing nutrient solution from the nutrient tank serves no purpose. This is a consequence of using one pump per nutrient tank. Nevertheless, you can just pump it back into the nutrient tank and flush out the beaker with purified water. Don't forget to dry the beaker if you have a heating coil.

This setup will allow you to adjust the pH up or down, make nutrient adjustments, perform hydrogen peroxide dosing at certain intervals, and assist with the purification of freshwater tanks before nutrients are added by introducing a chlorine-based solution, such as bleach.

In figure 7.4, there are nutrient solutions for only two phases, but you can add reservoirs for the fruiting mixture as well. As mentioned on page 61, nutrient mixtures will come in two separate parts to prevent the chemicals from interacting and forming insoluble sediments.

Putting all of this together will provide you with a complete lab system to automate most of the tasks you would otherwise have to do manually. Doing so will greatly reduce your daily involvement.

Nutrient Tank Manager

In this section I'll discuss how to automate the management of your nutrient tanks, starting with how to create a fresh batch of the nutrient mixture. You'll need to have at least one extra tank in your system that will be used to prepare new mixtures.

Use a solenoid valve to add water from your mains or from wherever you source your water. You can use a water sensor to detect when the tank is at the correct level, which should close the solenoid valve. Use the lab unit to add .07 ounces (2 ml) of the chlorine-based solution for every 1 quart (1 L) of water. This tank should have a UV light in it. Leave this on for twenty-four hours to break down the chlorine and assist with the purification process. After twenty-four hours, you can turn off the UV light and use the lab unit to add the correct concentration of nutrients to the tank. Remember to add each mixture one at a time and to run a water pump that falls back into the tank to help with circulation. An air stone will also speed up the process.

Take a TDS measurement and make adjustments if required. Once you have the correct ppm level, continue to cycle the mixture for up to thirty minutes. You can then measure the pH level and make the necessary adjustments. Cycle the solution for another thirty minutes before making any final pH adjustments.

At this point you'll have a new batch of nutrient solution. If this tank is elevated above the other nutrient tanks, you can drain it into the tank where it's supposed to go. If it's not elevated above the other nutrient tanks, you will need a water pump to pump it to the correct tank. Either way, you'll need a solenoid valve for each tank it goes to so you can direct the flow.

The nutrient tank should be cleaned before directing the new batch to it. Simply dispose of the old batch by using a solenoid valve and let it drain out naturally via a drainage pipe. Close the solenoid valve and rinse the tank. A good way to do this is to install a few 360-degree spraying nozzles inside each nutrient tank. They should spray up high enough to reach the top of the waterline when the tank is at full capacity. You don't need to add a full tank of water for the rinsing process, as a 10–20 percent level should be sufficient. You need to at least cover the water pump inlets.

While you are adding water, you can use the lab unit to add some hydroperoxide solution. Let it cycle for five minutes, and then flush out the tank. Add fresh water to the tank (5–10 percent) and rinse for another minute or two to flush out any remaining hydroperoxide. Finally, drain away the water. This will provide you with a clean tank. You can then introduce the new nutrient solution batch to the clean tank. You will likely need to clean the tank manually from time to time since buildup could form after a while.

If you need to switch out tanks, do so right after you have irrigated the crop and after most of the nutrient solution has drained back into the tank. You could even perform one last irrigation without any nutrients, using only your waterline. Of course, this would require an additional solenoid valve. Using only water will clear out any nutrient solution remaining in the growing medium and root area.

Draining, cleaning, and filling the tank could take about ten minutes, so you'll need to ensure that the crop can survive for this amount of time without irrigation. If you're using a water-retaining growing medium, such as coconut coir, this won't be a problem, and you can spend more time rinsing out the tank.

conclusion

I like gardening — it's a place where I find myself
when I need to lose myself.

ALICE SEBOLD

by now you should be fully versed in the field of hydroponics and should be comfortable enough to set up your own system, if you haven't done so already. Your hydroponic system can be as simple or as complicated as you want it to be; you've just got to take the first step. You can always begin with the most basic version to save on time and costs and expand on it later.

A good place to start would be with a micro greenhouse in which you have just one nutrient tank with one small A-frame or even a flat system. The micro greenhouse only needs to be big enough to enclose the system, and you can attach a hinge to the roof so you can gain access to it.

By using plastic sheeting and an inexpensive wooden frame, the cost of the micro greenhouse would be negligible. A basic PVC pipe system with a single water pump and air pump is also very affordable. You should be able to build an entry-level system for less than the cost of a new microwave oven, and you can easily finish the build in a weekend.

Even though this system will require daily involvement, it's the first step toward food security for you and your family. Since hydroponic systems are designed to be protected from environmental elements and allow you to create your own environmental conditions, you won't be as vulnerable as soil farmers, and you can even circumvent seasonal restrictions.

When you get to the point that your system is fully automated, you will begin to reap the most significant benefits of hydroponic farming. Even though the initial capital layout could be a bit higher, the long-term benefits will certainly be worth it.

A hydroponic system will be capable of producing food at a lower cost and a higher quality than food purchased from a store. The most important consideration is keeping down your recurring costs. The biggest ongoing expense will be grow lights, so if you mostly rely on natural light and only supplement when necessary, you'll be fine.

The field of hydroponics changes quickly since it readily embraces new technologies that can improve yields or assist with automation. Online resources will help you expand your current knowledge and stay up to date with the latest advancements.

Hydroponic farming is the future of food production, but there's no reason to wait for the rest of the world to catch up. Jump in and join others on the cutting edge who are already reaping the benefits of growing their own food.

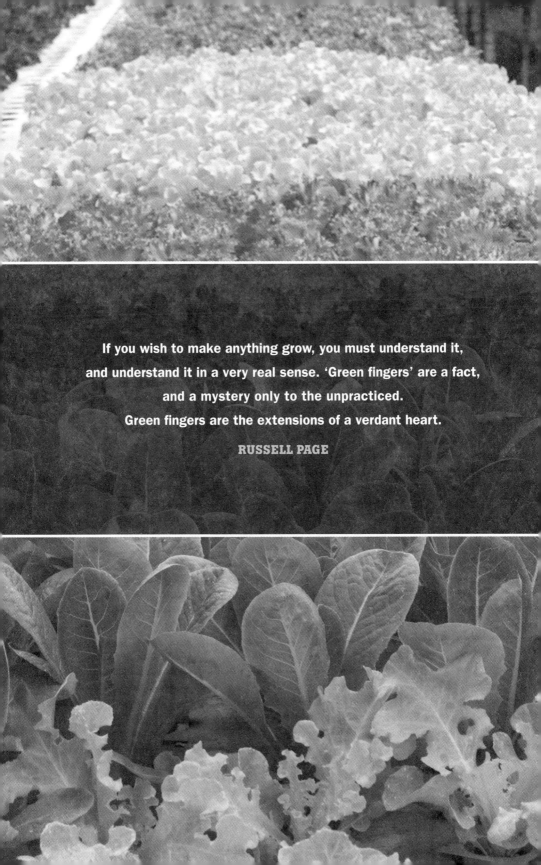

If you wish to make anything grow, you must understand it,
and understand it in a very real sense. 'Green fingers' are a fact,
and a mystery only to the unpracticed.
Green fingers are the extensions of a verdant heart.

RUSSELL PAGE

index

Cerreto Rossouw lives with his wife (and beloved cat) in the Helderberg area of Western Cape, South Africa. He is an entrepreneur at heart and showed interest in business and technol-

ogy at a very early age. During his younger years, he was always tinkering with electronics and taught himself computer programming at the age of ten. After school, Cerreto was briefly a computer science teacher but started to get involved in several business ventures where he used his program-

ming skills to gain the competitive edge. Most of these ventures were in the financial industry (banking, retail, investments, and the stock exchange). He is currently one of the founding owners of a successful and rapidly growing retail transaction switch that is operating in several countries.

Over the last decade, Cerreto has become interested in self-sustainability, especially when it involves new high-tech solutions and green technologies. As a South African citizen, he quickly learned that you can't always rely on basic services, such as water and electricity. Like many South Africans, circumstances forced him to come up with his own solutions, which led him to start researching alternative off-grid solutions. Although he's not completely off-grid yet, he has managed to implement multiple backup systems that might even lead to new future ventures.

During his research, Cerreto coincidentally came across the field of hydroponics and has been intrigued ever since. The use of hydroponics to aid in self-sustainability and the huge scope it has for high-tech implementations really piqued his interest. This led to the publishing of this book and a new hydroponic farming venture. For more information, visit hydroponicscropmanager.com.

GROUNDSWELL BOOKS

SOLUTIONS FOR A SUSTAINABLE WORLD

For more books that inspire readers to create a healthy,
sustainable planet for future generations, visit
BookPubCo.com

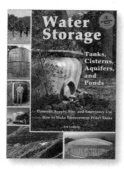

Water Storage

Art Ludwig

978-0-96434-336-8

$19.95

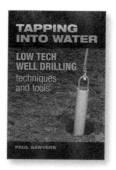

Tapping into Water

Paul Sawyers

978-1-57067-357-3

$15.95

*The New Create an Oasis
with Greywater, 6th Edition*

Art Ludwig

978-0-96434-333-7

$22.95

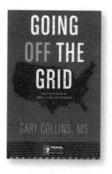

Going Off the Grid

Gary Collins, MS

978-1-57067-354-2

$14.95

Purchase these titles from your favorite book source or buy them directly from:
Book Publishing Company • PO Box 99 • Summertown, TN 38483 • 1-888-260-8458
Free shipping and handling on all orders